CW00348990

WORLD POLITICAL THEORIES

World Political Theories aims to change the way we think about non-Western political ideas. Each book in the series looks at a particular region or country, and how thinking about politics has developed there. In doing so, the books ask how universal political theory actually is, and to what extent place makes a difference. Through looking at the historical development of political thinking, the books provide important context for understanding contemporary politics, whilst introducing fresh ideas and challenges to conventional political theory.

TITLES ALREADY PUBLISHED

Patrick Chabal, *Africa: The Politics of Suffering and Smiling*
Shahrough Akhavi, *The Middle East: The Politics of the Sacred and Secular*

FORTHCOMING TITLES

Gurpreet Mahajan, *India: Cross-Cultural Conversations*

ABOUT THE AUTHOR

TONGDONG BAI is a professor at Fudan University in Shanghai. He holds a BS degree (nuclear physics) and an MA degree (philosophy of science) from Peking University, and a PhD degree (philosophy) from Boston University. He was an associate professor of philosophy at Xavier University in Cincinnati. His most recent books are: *A New Mission of an Old State: Classical Confucian Political Philosophy in a Contemporary and Comparative Context* and *Tension of Reality: Einstein, Bohr, and Pauli in the EPR Debates* (both in Chinese). His research is focused on the contemporary relevance of traditional Chinese political philosophy.

CHINA

The political philosophy of the Middle Kingdom

TONGDONG BAI

Zed Books
LONDON & NEW YORK

China: The Political Philosophy of the Middle Kingdom was first published in 2012 by
Zed Books Ltd, 7 Cynthia Street, London N1 9JF, UK and
Room 400, 175 Fifth Avenue, New York, NY 10010, USA

www.zedbooks.co.uk

FSC
www.fsc.org
MIX
Paper from
responsible sources
FSC® C013604

Designed and typeset in Monotype Joanna
by illuminati, Grosmont
Cover designed by Lucy Morton @ illuminati
Index by John Barker
Printed by CPI Group (UK) Ltd, Croydon CR0 4YY

Distributed in the USA exclusively by Palgrave Macmillan, a division of
St Martin's Press, LLC, 175 Fifth Avenue, New York, NY 10010, USA

A catalogue record for this book is available from the British Library
Library of Congress Cataloging in Publication Data available

ISBN 978 1 78032 076 2 hb
ISBN 978 1 78032 075 5 pb

Contents

Acknowledgements

I would like to thank Zed Books for publishing this fascinating series of world political theories and for asking me to write this short book on traditional Chinese political philosophy. I am particularly grateful to my editor, Ken Barlow, for his kind support, patience and helpful comments.

Many people have been instrumental in the formation of my outlook on traditional Chinese political philosophy; they are too numerous to thank here. However, special thanks are due to Daniel Bell, for his never-ending support for my work, for offering me his insights on many political issues, and for his comments on an earlier draft of this book.

Some of the material in this book is based on previously published work (Bai 2011 and Bai 2009b; the latter in turn being based on articles, including Bai 2008a, 2008b, 2008c, 2009a and 2009c). The English (and revised) version of Bai 2009b is now being considered for publication as well. I thank all the journals and presses that have published my works for their support. I have already expressed gratitude to those who offered criticisms of these works, so will not repeat these acknowledgements here.

The research for this book was supported by the Program for Professor of Special Appointment (Eastern Scholar) at Shanghai Institutions of Higher Learning, the 'New Century Excellent Talents in University' grant, Shanghai Educational Development Foundation (Shuguang Project), the 'Pujiang Talents' grant from the Shanghai government, the Shanghai Philosophy and Social Sciences Projects, and by research grants from Fudan University (the Guanghua program, 985 Project 2011RWXKZD009, 985 Project 2011RWXKZD010 and others). I am grateful for their support.

Introduction

Message from China

China is rising, but both Chinese and non-Chinese are wondering what message this rise offers. What do the Chinese want from the world? What can they give to the world? Many of those non-Chinese who perceive China's rise as a threat and those Chinese who hold grievances over the wrongs that the Western and Japanese colonial powers inflicted upon China in the late nineteenth and twentieth centuries believe that the Chinese want to revive the country's power and then take revenge for those wrongs. If this is the case, the world will be in a big trouble. Others believe that the rise of China may offer alternatives to the received economic and political models, which have been shown to be increasingly problematic.[1] Therefore the message of the rise of China has become an issue that haunts not only academic researchers but also concerned citizens the world over.

This book is intended to address these concerns by examining the traditional political thought of China. Before I explain how the book sets out to address these concerns, let me make clear what this book is not. It does not answer directly empirical questions such as

'Why has China risen again in today's world?' and 'Does the rise of China offer a model for economics and politics?' These issues are important, but they are beyond my competence, as a philosopher. Indeed, if history teaches us anything, it counsels that a measure of humility is required in dealing with such questions.

Let us consider an example. In *The Protestant Ethic and the Spirit of Capitalism* (1958), Max Weber, one of the most important sociologists and influential thinkers of the twentieth century, considers the Protestant ethic one of the factors that promotes capitalism; the implication (drawn by many East Asians) seems to be that Confucianism is, then, a reason for the lack of indigenous capitalistic development in East Asia. In consequence, the 'Westernizers' in East Asia have tried to rid East Asia of Confucianism so as to embrace capitalism and modernity. However, then East Asia rose while apparently still preserving many of its values, a fact that seems to debunk the allegedly Weberian thesis. As a result, it can be argued that Confucianism can actually promote the development of capitalism. This thesis carries its own risk, unfortunately. Indeed, after the Southeast Asian financial crisis, advocates of the 'Asian Model' suddenly became quiet.

There is a more dramatic example. During the height of Japan's apparently unstoppable rise to economic dominance, Harvard professor Ezra Vogel published *Japan as Number One: Lessons for America* (1979). Nowadays, however, the USA is more likely to go to Japan for lessons not in development, but in how to avoid stagnation.

The general historical lesson is that, first, we should be circumspect in our drawing of empirical conclusions from a vastly complicated world; second, if a culture takes a free ride from the economic rise, it will take a free fall when the economy goes bust.

It is now a popular practice to draw lessons from China's economic rise that may be useful to the world, just as people liked to do from Japan's economic rise a few decades back. This exercise carries risks. For example, many argue that Confucianism has played an important role in the rise of China and the rest of East Asia. They take it for granted that Confucian values are still dominant in the region.

But this is not self-evidently the case, especially in contemporary China.

First, other influential values played their part in traditional Chinese culture, such as those of Daoism, Buddhism and Legalism. Consider the common impression that Chinese culture historically has disparaged commerce. Taking it as the core of this culture, people tend to hold Confucianism responsible for this undervaluation. However, as this book will show, early Confucians were not against commerce and money-making. If blame lies anywhere, it is with some Daoists and Legalists, who did indeed hold a rather low opinion of commerce.

Second, in the first thirty years or so following the Communist revolution in China, the Chinese witnessed – and perpetrated – large-scale destruction of traditional values, which led some scholars to wonder whether a period of thirty years was greater than 5,000 years (popularly considered the duration of Chinese civilization). Indeed, Chinese traditional culture has been under attack since the famous May Fourth Movement (if not earlier). Traditional political institutions, social networks, and so on, have disappeared for good, a fact that led the Chinese historian Yu Yingshi 余英时 to call Confucianism a 'wandering soul' (because its 'body' – its institutional and social foundation – has been destroyed), and led another historian, John Makeham, to call Confucianism in contemporary academic discourse 'the lost soul' (Yu 2004b: 262–5; Makeham 2008).

The second thirty years and more of Communist rule (the reform, or capitalization, era) have also posed challenges to traditional culture. For example, radical urbanization has created a large migrant workforce. This has involved a growing break with traditional family structures (because many young people from rural areas no longer live at home with their extended families), on the basis of which traditional culture built its ascendancy.

Failure to understand these changes and their implications in recent Chinese history may also contribute a widespread misunderstanding in the West. There are regular news reports in the Western media concerning the suppression of Tibetan culture by the Han

Chinese (who constitute the majority of the Chinese people). This alleged suppression is often portrayed in racial or ethnic terms. However, generally speaking, the Western idea of nationality, in the sense of race, was alien to the Chinese throughout much of their history. More importantly, in the first thirty years of Communist rule, the Han Chinese did far more damage to their own culture (e.g. destruction of Confucian temples and of many other cultural heritage sites and institutions) than they did to Tibetan temples. In fact, much of the destruction of Tibetan temples was perpetrated by Tibetan radicals. So, the issue was not really racial or ethnic, but rather about radical modernizers versus traditionalists. In the course of the second thirty-year period, Tibetan culture has been threatened by commercialization, and many of the businesspeople are Han Chinese (though some are Tibetans). Yet, this is merely part of a vast trend of commercialization in China, and Han Chinese, being closer to the outside world, happen to have led it. Much of their activity has done great damage to Han Chinese culture as well. Thus the Tibetan issue is not really an ethnic issue, which Western journalists, perhaps coloured by their own history of ethnically based colonialism and suppression, fail to see.

A humorous comment, though of course exaggerating the situation, serves as an apposite observation on what is going on, value-wise, in China. According to the American journalist Adam Davidson, a US businessman once said that China 'was so huge and was changing so fast that everything you heard about it was true, and so was the opposite' (Davidson 2012).

Third, and related to the second issue, some factors that helped China in its miraculous growth trajectory are clearly not Confucian. An example is the government's ability to conduct demolitions that show little regard for the interests of the people directly involved, but that, nevertheless, might help to promote the long-term interest of the state and of the many at the sacrifice of the interests of the few. Empirical studies suggest that East Asians might think differently from Westerners, such as valuing material needs higher than

abstract rights and democracy.[2] But such differences could be the
result of economic development. So-called East Asian values could
be a consequence of the work ethic of the poor and needy, who
are likely to consider food and shelter more important than certain
abstract rights, or they could be the values of a more agrarian people
– China, and East Asia generally, has a higher percentage of poor and
agrarian people than the West. More importantly, these values are
hardly Confucian. For example, a pupil asked Confucius: if we had
to choose between food and trust among people, which one should
we give up? Confucius answered:

> Give up food. Death has always been with us since the beginning
> of time, but when there is no trust the common people will not be
> able to stand on their feet. (*Analects* 12.7)[3]

So clearly for Confucius, there are values higher than food and shelter,
in contrast to the alleged East Asian values that claim otherwise.

Therefore, although it is extremely important to identify what
cultural elements have contributed to China's economic rise, to
help us draw the appropriate lessons, we should first acknowledge
the risks involved in accepting such accounts. I believe that current
empirical studies of the political, sociological, and cultural reality
of contemporary China are still wanting, and more in-depth studies
are required before we can pass reliable judgement on the factors
informing China's economic rise. In the absence of such studies,
attempts to pin down these factors, although they may appear to be
based on the facts, may in reality be mistaken.

As a philosopher, I choose to stay on safer ground and focus on
the dominant political thought in China's past. In particular, I focus
on thinkers' normative messages; that is, on their views regarding
what the world ought to be like. This practice, I believe, has not
only theoretical significance but practical implications.

First, the various accounts offered in this book do not merely
describe the Chinese mind, but are meant to be universal. Traditional
Chinese political thinkers didn't consider their works a form of

'cultural studies'. Rather, they were envisioning an ideal political regime for every civilized people in the world. Indeed, the original terms for Chinese, *hua* 华 or *xia* 夏, don't signify a particular race, but simply the civilized people. In this sense, 'Chinese philosophy' is the philosophy for all civilized peoples; the 'Chinese' in the narrow sense happened to be the only known civilized people at the time the early Chinese thinkers were writing.

Second, regardless of how the Chinese thinkers envisioned their own teachings, we can still question whether they are philosophical. As I argue below, they are indeed philosophical. For me, philosophy deals with issues that transcend a particular time, a particular location and a particular people. Thus, to claim that these Chinese thoughts are philosophical means that they are dealing with issues that are not limited to one people in one area at one time. Throughout this book, we will see ideas of Chinese thinkers that echo those of Western thinkers. To understand traditional Chinese political philosophy, then, is not merely to understand how a particular group of people thinks, but to understand how wise and profound people in the past, be they Chinese, Greek or Indian, dealt with the issues we still have to deal with today. Thus, the process will help us deepen our understanding of many contemporary political issues. Throughout the book, I indicate points of comparison and contrast between Chinese thinkers and Western thinkers, as much as space allows in a short study. I hope that, as a result, the reader won't fall into the trap of indulging in the construction of simple 'stereotypes' – that is, the belief that 'the Chinese think this way, whereas the Westerners think that way'.[4] We will see that there is a diversity of thought among Chinese thinkers. Indeed, the differences among them may be greater than alleged differences between Chinese and Western thought. Likewise, often a Chinese thinker will be more successful at finding a kindred spirit in the West than among his fellow Chinese thinkers.

Therefore philosophy qua philosophy is relevant to different peoples from different areas at different times. In order to help the reader see this, on the basis of understanding how traditional Chinese thinkers thought, I occasionally ask questions such as, 'What would x say to this or that problem of today?', and 'What would x say if they witnessed contemporary democratic regimes?'

Moreover, as I argue in Chapter 1, there is another reason for the contemporary relevance of traditional Chinese thought: the Chinese political philosophers I focus upon, the pre-Qin thinkers, lived through transitions (roughly from 700 BCE to 200 BCE) comparable in many aspects to the European modernizations that occurred some two thousand years later. If this bold thesis stands, it will render further support to the contemporary and universal relevance of traditional Chinese political philosophy. For, from the very beginning the thought has dealt with issues of modernity, like those we still have to deal with today. Many political proposals offered by these Chinese thinkers echo, and perhaps influenced, European modern thinkers' ideas, as we will see.

Notwithstanding the many similarities, there are nevertheless significant points of difference between what the Chinese thinkers offered and what the modern European thinkers did. Throughout Chinese political history, many institutions and regimes rooted in traditional Chinese political philosophy were introduced and tested, some similar to and others different from the institutions and regimes put to the test by modern European states. As such they should be considered as paradigms competing to address the issues of modernity – that is, competing both among themselves and with Western models. They offer us precious points of reflection on contemporary political issues, and their successes and failures may shed light on current problems. Perhaps, after all, history has not come to an end in the Western form of liberal democracy, as the political theorist Francis Fukuyama famously claimed (1992). Instead there might be better models for human beings living in modern times than today's liberal democratic form of polity. But we will only be able to discover them if we adopt a perspective beyond the experience of Western modernity and its paradigms. If we are tempted to dismiss possible alternatives on the basis of the recent success of liberal democracy, we should remember the experience of the Chinese, who had far greater reason to dismiss other paradigms, given that China dominated the world economy for hundreds, if not thousands, of years.[5] For in hindsight we see that the Chinese were fatally mistaken in their hubris, which led to defeat and devastation after China encountered the industrialized and colonizing West. We run the risk of repeating this folly if we once again allow ourselves to subscribe to theories of the end of history.

As a consequence of Western hubris – its unswerving belief in the ultimate supremacy of liberal democracy – Chinese political philosophy has been largely neglected by Westerners for the past hundred years or so. Chinese intellectuals who are overwhelmed by the success of the West share in this neglect. Indeed, even the so-called 'cultural conservatives', among them the New Confucians of the twentieth century, only focus on the ethical aspect of traditional Chinese philosophy, their implicit or explicit assumption being that there is little to learn from traditional Chinese political philosophy and from regimes which, for them, produced only a failed state. This book, in contrast, is one of the few works to focus on traditional Chinese political philosophy. It is hoped that the reader will find merit in this philosophy.

The book offers not only a historical account of traditional Chinese political philosophy, but also some normative ideas that may help us reflect productively on the world's problems today. In addition to addressing matters of universal or global concern, however, I also wish to offer readers some understanding of the Chinese mind. Although, as I have argued, it is a risky enterprise to identify cultural elements that have contributed to China's rise (or its problems), nonetheless one of the first steps to achieving this understanding is to appreciate the richness and complexity of thought in the schools of traditional Chinese political philosophy. In this way we can hope to avoid making the mistake of attributing to a thought what is actually alien to it. As we have seen, people attribute the denigration of commerce to

Confucianism. One simple reason for this (mis)understanding is their lack of appreciation of Confucian teachings. Moreover, even though it is hazardous to speculate on which school of traditional thought plays how much of a role in traditional Chinese culture, it is safe to say that certain dominant schools of thought have historically constituted, and may still constitute, the undercurrent of the Chinese mind. Thus, understanding such traditional political thought can help us grasp what is going on in the country today.

In short, then, by offering an understanding of the ideas and political institutions of China's past, this book also provides a normative assessment of contemporary global issues and an insight into the Chinese mind. That is, it has both a normative and a descriptive function, a universal ambition and the intention of helping the reader understand a particular country and its people. Hopefully, the book will contribute to a better understanding of the past and the present and to bringing about a better future.

Overview

There are many schools of traditional Chinese political philosophy. Given the limits of space, however, I will focus only on those that have had a long-standing influence on traditional Chinese politics and political thought: namely, Confucianism, Legalism and Daoism. As for other known schools of traditional Chinese thought, Mohism 墨家 was a dominant school in the pre-Qin era; according to common understanding it advocated equality and universal love. But it entered oblivion following the Qin dynasty (221–206 BCE). Many religions have been introduced into China, such as Buddhism, Islam, Zoroastrianism, and various sects of Christianity, but only Sinicized Buddhism – that is, Chinese Buddhism – has become a part of the mainstream culture, although its direct influence is more ethical than political.

Moreover, it is not possible to consider all historical developments of the three schools of political philosophy in this short book. Instead I will focus on their early manifestations, as they were developed in the pre-Qin era. The writings in this era had a more direct access to the problems at hand, rather than being concerned with commenting on earlier works. They thus possessed a greater immediacy. Furthermore, they constitute the root of Chinese political thought, and to have knowledge of the root is crucial for an understanding of the tree.

In Chapter 1, before considering the three schools, I first describe the world in which the early Chinese thinkers lived, and the problems this world posed to them. To understand the problems that concern a school of philosophy is the foremost task in studying the work of that school, as the sophisticated systems and technical concepts are only invented in order to address them. I show that the world of early Chinese thinkers was one in transition to early modernity, and in this sense they were Moderns, and not Ancients, in Western idiom.

After clarifying the historical background and showing the problems facing early Chinese thinkers, I first explore Confucianism. Confucius was perhaps the first private teacher in Chinese history; all other schools of political thought can be traced back to him. Those sympathetic to Daoism may object, because they believe that the author of the book *Lao Zi* lived before Confucius. Sidestepping this controversial issue, I formulate the political teachings of the *Lao Zi* as a critique of Confucianism.

As I argue in Chapter 1, the crucial problems brought about by early Chinese modernization are: the need to create a social glue for a large, populous, and well-connected state; the formation of a new post-feudal ruling class; and the issue of international relations – in particular, the problem of 'world' peace among Chinese states.

Chapter 2 considers early Confucians' answers to the problems of social glue and international relations. The key is their introduction of concepts such as 'humanity' and 'compassion'. I explain these ideas, and flesh out their political implications for issues both then and now, such as how and why compassion can function as a social glue; the relations between the private and the public; international relations and just wars; and issues connected to rights, environmentalism and feminism.

Chapter 3 focuses on early Confucians' response to the need to form a new ruling class. I show how they offered a new foundation for the legitimacy of the sovereign and tried to build a hierarchical political structure on the basis of equality and mobility. I argue that their ideal regime, adjusted to today's reality, may serve to address political issues more effectively than liberal democracy.

I am sympathetic to Confucianism as a political philosophy. And it may be that the apparently charitable reading of the thought in Chapters 2 and 3, in contrast to occasional harsh criticisms of today's ideologies, will lead some readers to doubt my commitment to objectivity. However, such is not a straightforward reflection of my own philosophical preferences. For, to the reader today many Confucian ideas appear to be politically incorrect; I therefore consider it my job as a philosopher to defend an alien doctrine as well as I can. This is important, maybe crucial, in opening our minds to what we may well experience as alien teaching. Accustomed to today's mainstream ideas as many readers are, it would be all too easy to respond with a knee-jerk rejection of Confucianism and the other unfamiliar thinking under discussion, including their critiques of contemporary ideas. My aim, therefore, is to present the best case for them, and in this I can only ask for the reader's indulgence. Moreover, as the other two schools I consider are formulated partly as reactions to Confucianism, it follows that the ground must be well laid before we can move on. Although in these two chapters I refrain from criticizing Confucian ideas, in the following chapters, by introducing different schools of thought and by explaining and defending their criticisms of Confucianism, I offer some critical evaluation of Confucian ideas.

Chapter 4 looks at Daoism, and examines how it addressed the two pressing issues of the day. Its answers are contrasted with those offered in early Confucianism. Consideration is given to why early Daoists found the Confucian responses problematic and held their own to be superior. Thereafter I offer some criticisms of this school of thought.

In Chapter 5, I move on to examine Legalism. The thinkers in question, notably Han Fei Zi, came after both the early Confucians and the early Daoists, hence they are considered last. Moreover, Han Fei Zi's thought echoes ideas of the *Lao Zi*, and is highly critical of Confucianism. Thus it was necessary to acquaint the reader first with the thinking of the other two schools in order to appreciate the work of Han Fei Zi and to place his thought. Again, at the end of the chapter I offer some criticisms of Legalist teachings.

In the course of discussing the three philosophical traditions, I consider where appropriate their theoretical interaction and discuss their influence on Chinese political institutions in the generations to come. Chapter 6 then focuses more closely on these issues, in particular how the ideas came to influence traditional Chinese politics, both separately as movements of thought and in combination. Their successes and failures are assessed, further revealing the merits and problems with the schools of thought, and helping us reach a deeper understanding of traditional Chinese politics.

Throughout the entire discussion, implicit and explicit comparisons and contrasts are drawn with Western political philosophy, especially its modern forms and contemporary ideological expressions, and the relevance of these traditional Chinese political teachings today is asserted, on occasion through their reconstruction within a present-day context. In the concluding chapter, a summary of the arguments is given, so as to lead the reader to ponder upon the central concern of the book: what kind of regime is the best for human beings in modern times?

How Chinese philosophers express themselves

Before I move on to discuss traditional Chinese thought, let me first clarify how Chinese political philosophers express themselves, which is vital for an understanding of the ways they are read. Traditional Chinese philosophers express themselves differently from their Western counterparts — which could be one reason why many people deny that there is such a thing as Chinese political philosophy.[6] Many, indeed most, traditional Chinese philosophical texts are written not in the form of treatises, but as records of dialogues, perhaps between a master and his pupils; as aphorisms; as concrete political advice to rulers or as policy debates with other ministers or counsellors; and as commentaries on classical texts or historical events. Therefore they do not contain argumentation that is as extensive and systematic as most works of Western political philosophy.[7] They are often not written for the purpose of purely theoretical discourse, and thus lack an apparent system and that sense of detachment and universality. One important reason for this, as the Chinese historian Qian Mu 钱穆 pointed out, is that from the so-called Spring and Autumn period (which began around 770 BCE) on, the Chinese intellectual elite had the opportunity to become part of the ruling elite, a situation sharply different from that pertaining in medieval Europe (Qian Mu 2005: 21). The Chinese intellectual elite in the past could thus put their political thoughts and theories into practice, and had little need to work them up into theories detached from practice. In fact, the political philosopher Jean-Jacques Rousseau made a point that supports Qian Mu's observation in the opening paragraphs of *On the Social Contract*:

> I shall be asked if I am a prince or a legislator, to write on politics. I answer that I am neither, and that is why I do so. If I were a prince or a legislator, I should not waste time in saying what wants doing; I should do it, or hold my peace. (Rousseau 1978: 46)

Of course, this defence only explains why the writings of many Chinese political writers are different from those in the Western tradition, and suggests that, if given the opportunity (or the lack of opportunity in real-world politics), these Chinese writers could have written works that bear more resemblance in style to the writings in the Western tradition. But it should be noted that the lack of apparent formal system doesn't mean that there is no real yet implicit system in Chinese political writing. Indeed, in the Chinese commentary tradition the reader is required to 'connect the dots' and grasp the implicit system of ideas within the Chinese classics. This exercise can be very rewarding because, although their works lack leisurely speculations, many political writers of traditional China – including most of the thinkers whose works are discussed in this book – recorded in their works much first-hand experience of politics at the highest level.

Moreover, to claim that Chinese classical texts are not philosophical because they do not contain as much argumentation as Western philosophical works is based upon the unexamined assumption that argumentation is the only way of philosophizing. If we take philosophy as reflections on and examinations of common human experiences, and if it is the case that there are different ways for these reflections and examinations to be expressed, we can consider a work as of philosophy even if it contains little argumentation. Furthermore, the aphoristic and dialogical format of many Chinese classics may be taken as an implicit form of argumentation, an argument sketch, with only the important steps and key or difficult points made explicit and with the detail – that the reader is required to supply – left out. As Friedrich Nietzsche put it, 'In the mountains the shortest way is from peak to peak: but for that one must have long legs. Aphorisms should be peaks – and those who are addressed, tall and lofty' (Nietzsche 1954: 40).

To sum up, traditional Chinese political thought should be considered political philosophy. For it involves reflections upon and examinations of political problems that are, I would argue, universal and timeless among human societies. The universality of these problems will be shown when we come to look at the issues with which traditional Chinese philosophers were dealing. Indeed, I would further argue that, in cases where issues of concern to a group of people are particular to that group, they should be considered cultural issues, and therefore are the proper subject of anthropology, not of philosophy. Shared and common problems are the reason for us to study different schools of political philosophy. At the same time, a school must have something distinctive in order to justify our study of it. Traditional Chinese political philosophy is deserving of study not only because it often expresses itself in ways distinct from many Western political philosophical texts, but because it sometimes offers different solutions to common political problems. For a philosophy to be worth studying, we might say, it has to be both the same as (in terms of issues) and different from (in terms of its approaches to these issues) another philosophy.

However, the distinctive ways in which Chinese political philosophers have expressed themselves pose a challenge to the reader. Recovering and understanding the intended meaning of their texts demand more of the reader than Western philosophical texts written in the form of treatises.[8] To make the matter even more challenging, early Chinese texts, like Ancient Greek texts, are often corrupted in places, and tend not to have punctuation. Hence the reader must decide whether and in which way the text is corrupted, and how to punctuate it. Decisions on these matters can lead to different readings of the text in question. Obviously, short and aphoristic texts are the most difficult to punctuate and make sense of. But such work is not lacking in rigour. Related sources, such as the information we have about the author(s) and about his/her/their claims elsewhere, authoritative commentaries, and so forth, can help direct our speculations regarding the meaning, and thus the punctuation, of the text in question. Nonetheless, the interpretation of many earlier Chinese texts remain controversial – a point the reader should bear in mind when considering the interpretations offered in this book (note that, for stylistic reasons, I avoid equivocation – 'might,' 'may', 'perhaps' – even though many of my readings contain speculative elements).

ONE

Modernity before its time: the historical context of 'classical' Chinese political thought

Political thought in traditional China flourished during the so-called Spring and Autumn and Warring States periods (SAWS for short, roughly from 770 to 222 BCE). As was argued in the Introduction, to understand the political thought in this era we need first to recognize the problems that defined these times. In this chapter, therefore, I offer a summary of the historical background of traditional Chinese thought. In particular, I explain the transitions that took place during the SAWS, and thus outline the issues early Chinese political thinkers faced. These discussions will lay the foundation of our investigations of different schools of early Chinese political philosophy in later chapters. I argue that the dramatic transitions China experienced during the SAWS were similar to the European transition to modernity, and established the basic political framework for the following two thousand years of Chinese history. The early Chinese political philosophers, then, were addressing the issues thrown up during this epoch of change. Some of their answers would guide subsequent transitions and exert influence on future regimes in traditional China.

Historical background

Our first task is to understand the changes China experienced during the SAWS. There were legendary founding fathers and sage rulers in Chinese history, such as the Yellow Emperor (often said to be the initiator of Chinese civilization), Yao, Shun and Yu. The sage ruler Yao was said to have given up his throne to the unrelated sage ruler Shun. Shun did likewise, giving up the throne to Yu. But then a son of Yu's inherited the throne, thus starting the first dynasty in China, the Xia (2070–1600 BCE), in which the kings came from Yu's bloodline. That said, whether these figures were indeed real historical characters, the dates of the Xia dynasty, and the accuracy of the stories that have passed down, are all controversial questions among historians. Less so is the existence of the second dynasty, the Shang (seventeenth–eleventh centuries BCE). The last king of the Xia dynasty, King Jie, was said to be a tyrant, who was overthrown by the founding father of the Shang dynasty, King Tang. A few hundred years later, history repeated itself, only this time it was the last king of Shang, King Zhou, who was the alleged tyrant; King Wu overthrew Zhou, and thus the Shang line, and founded the Zhou dynasty in the middle of the eleventh century BCE. Again, the historical record is far from adequate; indeed the authenticity and reliability of the extant documentation remain in doubt. Nevertheless, the reader must have a sense of the history that led to the periods on which this book will focus. Importantly, many of the figures and events described so far resurface in the works of the 'hundred schools'.

The Zhou dynasty was divided into two periods, or 'sub-dynasties'. The first period is the so-called Western Zhou dynasty (mid-eleventh century–771 BCE). The political structure of this dynasty was a feudalistic, pyramid-like and expanding system. The kings of Zhou (especially of the first generation) enfeoffed their relatives, loyal and competent ministers (many of whom were also relatives), nobles of the past Shang dynasty, and so on. These people became the princes of their own principalities. Some of these principalities were in the remote areas of the empire, functioning in effect as colonies in otherwise 'barbarous' areas (Qian 1996: 57).[1] The establishment and expansion of these de facto colonies thus helped to broaden the imperial reach. When the principalities expanded, their rulers did the same as the kings did, enfeoffing their own relatives and ministers. Across the entire empire, the king ruled over princes (of various ranks), princes ruled over lesser lords, and so on. At each level, one master ruled over a limited number of subjects, enabling rule through personal influence, blood relations, contracts between rulers and their subjects, and codes of conduct.

The last king of the Western Zhou dynasty turned out to be a bad king because he neglected his duties and used his power frivolously. The Zhou capital was ransacked by a tribe of 'barbarians', assisted by the disgruntled ruler of a feudal state, and the king was killed. The next king had to establish a new capital east of the older capital; hence this new period of the Zhou dynasty is called Eastern Zhou (770–256 BCE). The era from the beginning of the Eastern Zhou dynasty to the establishment of the next dynasty, the Qin, is also divided into two periods, the Spring and Autumn (770–476 BCE) and the Warring States (476–222 BCE) periods.[2] During the SAWS, the aforementioned hierarchical system began to collapse: familial bonds and contractual and ritual relations had weakened after generations; the empire had expanded to what would be its limit and population growth had put pressure on the limited resources, which made infighting inevitable. In the Spring and Autumn period, the king of Zhou was paid only nominal homage, and eventually the boundaries of the principalities ceased to be respected. Through wars and conquests, seven large and independent states emerged. This was the beginning of the Warring States period, in which the nominal king of Zhou was eventually removed from his throne. At this time, rulers had to rule directly over states that were becoming ever larger and more populous, and the survival of both states and rulers depended upon their physical strength alone.

Similarities between China during the SAWS and Europe's transition to modernity

The transitions experienced by the Chinese states during the SAWS bear some uncanny similarities to the European transition from the Middle Ages to (Western) modernity. The political system in the Middle Ages was also a feudalistic, pyramid-like structure. Every level of the ruling structure was a de facto small state with a small population, and the bonds were likewise a combination of contractual, ritual and blood relations. This structure, too, was collapsing during the transition to Western modernity. The emerging large and populous states were fighting ('warring') for domination. Of course there are differences. For example, there were Ancient Greek and Roman civilizations long before the Middle Ages, which served as invaluable philosophical, political and cultural resources during the European transition to modernity. The Chinese people in the period of the SAWS might have had a stronger sense of cultural and political identity and continuity than Europeans did during their transition, thanks to imagined or real memories of China's past and the efforts of some past Zhou rulers.[3] There was no secular throne in medieval Europe with the status of overlordship as high, long-standing and stable as that enjoyed by the kings of Western Zhou. The papacy was relatively stable, but whether it can be seen as an explicit overlordship similar to the role played by the kings of Western Zhou is debatable. A driving economic force in China's transition was an agricultural revolution (the widespread use of iron, etc.), though this was less drastic than the commercial revolution that occurred at the beginning of the Western transition and was certainly dwarfed by the Industrial Revolution that came towards the end. The European transition to modernity was accompanied by a territorial expansion into Africa and the Americas, while Chinese civilization during the SAWS reached the territorial limit imposed by economic, political and technological conditions. The European 'warring states' did not manage to achieve the kind of unity that the Chinese states achieved, although they did manage to wage two 'world' wars, among many other, smaller-scale, military conflicts.[4]

Nevertheless, the similarities between the SAWS transition and the Western modernization are clear and profound. Gone, along with the feudal system, were the noble classes and their way of life and politics. During the SAWS, exclusive inheritance of land by the noble class was abolished, along with the old communal system; a free market in land emerged. The West saw the notorious enclosure movement in England. The military became plebeianized, and so the nobles' codes of conduct vanished. Wars served the naked needs of the economic struggle for resources, and became a brutal sport of beheading. As Qian Mu observes, compared to wars in the Spring and Autumn period, when the feudal system was tottering but still in place, those in the Warring States period were downright savage and ugly (Qian 1996: 88–9). Correspondingly, Europe saw the outbreak of Napoleon's people's war, and the large-scale killing involved in all-out warfare. In this new form of war, wars were no longer confined to the nobles, and could involve everyone in a state. Thus the distinction between the military and innocent civilians became far more blurred than in the feudal age. This remains an issue to this day, still posing a serious challenge to the Geneva Convention, based as it is upon a strict separation of innocent citizenry and military.

Thus, while we must acknowledge the differences between the SAWS transition in China and that from the Middle Ages to modern times in Europe, there are nevertheless profound similarities between them. If the transition in the West is understood as 'modernization', then it follows that China had already experienced its own modernization of sorts, a few hundred years before the onset of the Common Era – that is, two thousand years before the West![5] This conclusion may help us to re-examine the notion of modernization, and to understand the nature of the distinctions between the Ancients and the Moderns. It also means that Chinese thinkers during the SAWS were already dealing with issues of modernity. It is to these that we now turn.

Nature and problems of modernity

In the feudal systems of China and Europe, each level of the pyramid-like ruling structure comprised only a small community of a few hundred or, at most, a few thousand people, bonded by certain rituals, codes of conduct, and explicit or implicit contracts. That is, the community on each level was a de facto small state, a community of acquaintances largely sharing the same values. After the transition to modernity these levels collapsed, and what emerged was large, populous, well-connected states composed of strangers. This might appear to be an insignificant change, but in politics 'size matters'. The pyramid-like feudal structure does not seem to have worked on a large scale over a long period of time because, after all, the number of trusted relatives and friends was likely to have been limited. More importantly, in a small community the noble codes of conduct and the virtues based upon a shared, comprehensive conception of the Good were likely to have been maintained. But when the community was too large to be considered as such, unless coercive means were employed, these codes and virtues could no longer serve as a social glue that bound the whole society together, and thus a pluralism of values became inevitable. This is a facet of pluralism understood by some Western modern thinkers, as it was by Chinese thinkers during the SAWS.[6]

In short, the point comes when the old political structure no longer has relevance to the new reality, and a new regime is desperately needed. The issues that need to be addressed are the following. First, what can replace the old virtues and become the new social glue for both the ruling class and society as a whole? Second, the ruling class that was built upon nobility by birth was seriously weakened, and the pyramid-like structure that was associated with it was gone. What should replace this form of governance? There are three sub-issues here. The first is that there were no international relations in feudalism. Come the emergence of independent states, how should such relations be handled? The second is that the legitimacy of the king of

Zhou was said to come from heaven (although, as we will see, this
'heaven' might already have been humanized in Western Zhou); the
legitimacy of lesser lords came from the approval of greater lords.
With this structure gone, what should provide the legitimacy for
rulership? The final sub-issue is related to the previous one. That is,
within each state, how should members of the ruling class, other
than the ruler, be selected? On the last question, there are similarities
between the answers offered by SAWS-era Chinese thinkers and those
offered by Enlightenment and modern thinkers in the West. These
latter, or most of them, advocated equality and mass education, while
the former, especially some early Confucians, argued for equality
among all human beings in terms of their potential to become wise
and virtuous, and likewise for some form of mass education. Both
groups believed that, under 'modern' conditions, upward mobility
was needed, so that the worthy among the masses are able to become
members of the ruling class, and have mobility within this class. But
the thinkers differ from each other on how this upward mobility
works. For example, the Legalist philosopher Han Fei Zi 韩非子
objected to Confucian education and to the Confucian meritocracy,
advocating instead a meritocracy based upon farming and military
achievement. Of course, not all thinkers embrace modernity. As
we will see, both the Lao Zi and Rousseau found modernity and its
consequences abhorrent, and called for a return to the pre-modern
times of small states with small populations.

The similarities of thought between Western modern thinkers and
Chinese thinkers of the SAWS era reflect the fact that they were con-
fronting similar problems. This in turn helps give us a new perspective
on the historical facts. For example, ideas from China once offered
political inspiration and ideals to certain Enlightenment thinkers.[7]
Clearly, the China they knew included imaginary elements, and they
probably intended China and praise for it as esoteric criticism of their
own regimes. But if this imagined China captures some aspects of
Chinese thinking on 'modernity', the reason that these ideas resonated
with those of European thinkers during the period of modernization

was likely because they addressed issues of direct concern to them. In historical studies, we know that the spread of innovations (technology, regime, etc.) may not have always been direct. For example, people who lacked a certain technology may have heard about it, and then proceeded to invent it 'independently'. Moreover, whether developed independently or not, an invention or a new regime can only become established if there is a new environment ready to receive it. Otherwise it will not last long, for the conditions will not exist for it to thrive.[8] From this historical point of view, we can say that Chinese thinking may have played a constructive role at the beginning of European modernization, and that such a role was not incidental but had profound reasons. More research needs to be done in this area, particularly concerning the basis and effect of China's influence at this time.[9] If the influence is shown to be constructive and not inadvertent, my thesis regarding China's early modernity and the nature of modernity stands to be further corroborated.

Another historical process whose understanding can be shaped by the notion of Chinese modernity is Japan's modernization. Before the Meiji restoration, Japan was heavily influenced by Chinese culture. This might suggest that the Japanese political system before the Meiji period was comparable to that in contemporary China. However, if we follow the understanding of feudalism and modernity offered in this chapter, it would be more accurate to say that since this Japanese political system was feudalistic, it was actually closer to the Chinese one during the Western Zhou dynasty or the transitional one during the Spring and Autumn era. The Meiji restoration, then, would be a combination of the Chinese transition to modernity (achieved by the unification of China under the rule of Qin, and not by the marginalized and subsequently abolished king's court of Zhou; this in contrast to the case of Japan, which was unified by the once marginalized king's court) and Western modernization, which carried with it industrialization and consequent technological advance.[10]

There are many theories of modernity, however, and it goes without saying that many would not accept the understanding outlined here. For example, if we consider Western European states, we may conclude that modernity consists of a market economy, equality, liberty, and the idea of the legitimacy of the sovereign, and reject the idea that what China experienced during the SAWS constituted modernization. To be clear, the thesis of China's early modernity does not maintain that there are no differences between Chinese and Western processes of modernization, but only that there are sufficient similarities. As mentioned, European modernization was fed by cultural resources from Ancient Greece and Rome that were not available in China. But even regarding the differences, we need to consider whether, in some cases, these might be merely apparent, with deeper similarities present that were perhaps the product of similar social changes.

For example, a market economy emerged and developed only gradually in the West; an important change during the SAWS was the marketization of land. Or let's consider equality, itself is a complicated concept. Some early Confucians argued that all human beings had equal potential, and promoted education that was not based upon class distinctions. The Legalist thinker Han Fei Zi also introduced the idea of equality before the law, with the exception of the ruler; likewise, at the dawn of European constitutionalism, monarchs were often beyond the law. The collapse of an aristocracy based on blood relations in China made possible a choice of career, which is a form of freedom or liberty. On the issue of the legitimacy of a sovereign, it should be made clear that in ancient times (Europe during the Middle Ages and China before the SAWS), although the sovereign of the state possessed legitimacy, this was held to come from divine will. So, what really distinguishes the Moderns from the Ancients is not legitimacy per se, but the requirement that this legitimacy not be the expression of divine will. This requirement relates to pluralism and equality, characteristics of modernity. In Max Weber's terms, there is a process of disenchantment in modernization. In the West, the new 'disenchanted' understanding of legitimacy is expressed through the idea of a social contract and democratic politics. In China, 'the mandate of heaven', a form of divine will, might already have been humanized in Western Zhou.[11] In a document allegedly from the Western Zhou period, it is claimed that 'Heaven hears through the ears of the people, and Heaven sees through the eyes of the people' ('Taishi' 泰誓 ('Great Declaration') of Shangshu 尚书 (The Book of Documents)). Confucians during the SAWS, especially Mencius, developed further the idea that the legitimacy of the sovereign comes from winning the hearts and minds of the people by satisfying their material and spiritual needs. Of course, there are differences in the expressions of modernity and the treatment of modern questions. But they could be differences in approach to similar problems rather than ideas and theories pertaining to problems that are incommensurable. Besides, secularization, which is often considered a vital and distinctive component of Western modernization, may have resulted from a combination or convergence of the fundamental changes shared by Chinese early modernization and European modernization, such as the demand for a new source of legitimacy for sovereign rule, the necessity of pluralism in a non-oppressive society, improvement in mass education, and so on, as well as from something unique to Europe, such as the fact that in medieval, feudal Europe, religion was an important social glue. That is, secularization may not have been a primary feature of modernization.

To be clear, the transition to modernity, in both China and Europe, was long and messy. During the SAWS, for instance, many states remained stuck in their old ways. Indeed only the state of Qin enacted what could be called a distinctive modernization programme. Likewise, in Europe, feudal elements existed in Russia into the early twentieth century. It is equally true that part of the process in Europe occurred in the late modern period and yet other aspects had to wait until the contemporary era. But this might simply tell us that sometimes the transition from the era of the Ancients to that of the Moderns takes time. After all, it took some 500 years for China to go through the entire transition, and it can in fact be argued that many historical events in China after SAWS were nonetheless still responses to challenges posed by 'modernity'.[12]

'Classical' Chinese political philosophy as modern philosophy

If we hold to the thesis that SAWS-era thinkers set out to address issues of modernity, then Chinese philosophical thought from that time should properly be categorized as modern. As indicated in the Introduction, many people maintain that there was no philosophy in traditional China – a position I reject. Others argue that traditional Chinese philosophy existed, and it is far closer to ancient and medieval Western philosophy than it is to modern Western philosophy.[13] That is, the distinction between traditional Chinese philosophy (which was being written well into the era of Western modernity) and modern Western philosophy is a distinction between ancient and modern philosophy.[14] Among those who hold to this view, some further argue that, based upon a progressive view of the discipline, Chinese philosophy represents a stage that Western philosophy has already transcended.[15] However, if, as I have argued, we understand philosophy as the attempt to answer questions eternal and integral to human existence that are at the same time ultimately unsolvable, this progressive view, which is partly influenced by belief in the progress of the modern sciences, becomes problematic. Still others argue that although Chinese philosophy can be seen as the equivalent of ancient and medieval Western philosophy, ancient thoughts are actually more profound than modern thoughts, thus strengthening the contemporary relevance of Chinese philosophy.[16] For me, this belief is just as problematic as the progressive dogma. In my view, whether a philosophy is relevant or not does not depend upon when it was formulated; rather, its depth lies precisely in its ability to remain relevant and withstand the test of time. Chinese philosophy, even if it were equivalent to ancient Western philosophy, is not necessarily inferior. More importantly, though, traditional Chinese philosophy should, I would argue, be categorized as modern philosophy. That is, traditional Chinese philosophy is relevant to contemporary problems not only because it is philosophy, and because philosophy qua philosophy has a timeless relevance, but also because it is a *modern* philosophy – meaning that at least some of the issues it addresses are particular to modernity and thus to the contemporary world.

Let us be more specific. G.W.F. Hegel and Max Weber are among those who have erroneously maintained that there is no such a thing as Chinese philosophy or dismissed it by labelling it ancient philosophy.[17] Even worse, due to the Chinese being dazzled by the achievements of the Western powers and, later, misguided by Chinese Communist ideology, a common label for traditional Chinese thought (Confucianism in particular), throughout the previous century into this one, is 'garbage from 2,000 years of feudalism and authoritarianism'. This claim is wrong on many levels. As we shall see, China transcended the stage of feudalism during the SAWS, after which the political regimes were not particularly feudalistic. Furthermore, they were not straightforwardly authoritarian either.

Others have held a more positive view of traditional Chinese philosophy. For example, the Western philosopher Karl Jaspers put SAWS-era Chinese thinking on a par with ancient Indian and Greek philosophy, labelling them together as the thought of the Axial Age (1953). And yet this formulation fails to capture the essence of Chinese thought during the SAWS, which, as I have said, more properly belongs to the work of the Moderns rather than the Ancients. The German scholar of Chinese philosophy Heiner Roetz similarly characterizes Chinese thought during that time as being of the Axial Age, thereby committing the same mistake as Jaspers (Roetz 1993). In short, since the SAWS Chinese political thinkers and politicians have been dealing with issues of modernity, and have experimented with different solutions both in theory and in practice. Thus traditional Chinese political thought should be considered an important resource to help us reflect upon the issues of modernity.

TWO

The middle way of Confucianism: humanity as the new social glue

Having explained the nature of the problems faced by early Chinese thinkers, I now turn to early Confucianism. As indicated earlier, there are two reasons to discuss early Confucianism before going into the other two schools to be considered. First, Confucius may well have been the first private teacher, thereby initiating what would become a tradition of non-official scholars, some of whom would in turn go on to found their own schools of political philosophy. Second, and more importantly, the other two schools will be formulated partly as critical responses to Confucian solutions to issues arising from China's modernity. In this chapter, I focus on early Confucians' responses to a pressing concern of the time, the need for a new social glue, and their implications for other issues of the day and our contemporary world, such as international relations and just war.

Confucius and his school

Among the philosophers of the SAWS era – the pre-Qin thinkers as they are usually called[1] – one group of thinkers who tried to address the problem of 'modernity' was the early Confucians, the most influential of whom were Confucius (551–479 BCE), Mencius (372–289 BCE) and Xun Zi (313–238 BCE).[2]

The English adjectival form 'Confucian' comes from Confucius, the 'founder' of this school. 'Confucius' is the Latinized form of the name Kong Zi,[3] 'Kong' being the family name, and 'Zi' meaning 'master'. Confucius belonged to the lineage of Shang kings, although the noble status was almost completely lost in his father's generation. Although his father was still an official of lower rank, his mother was perhaps a concubine of his father's. When Confucius was born his father was old; he died when the boy was about 3 years old. Confucius, then, grew up from a lowly and poor background. An official once asked one of Confucius's pupils why, if Confucius was a sage, he could do so many things (presumably believing that, being of noble lineage, he would lack the skills of a commoner). Whereas the pupil wanted to embellish his teacher's standing, Confucius himself was more forthcoming:

> How well the Tai Zai [the title of this official] knows me! I was of humble background when I was young, and was thus skilled in many lowly things. Should a junzi[4] be skilled in many things? No, not at all. (Analects 9.6)

In spite of his lowly background, Confucius became educated (he was partly self-taught), and developed political ambitions. He wished to restore order to his home state of Lu and to other states nominally under the Zhou king. At one point he rose to a high rank in Lu, and was in contact with rulers of other small states; but he did not hold on to any high position long enough to carry through his restoration plan. Instead, he journeyed from state to state, hoping to find a sympathetic ruler, but to no avail. In this sense, he was a failure in politics. His success came in cultivating a loyal group of followers, whom he tutored in matters hitherto reserved for the nobility. Confucius was China's first private teacher, and many of his pupils would follow his example. In consequence, almost all the pre-Qin philosophical schools trace their lineage back to Confucius – although many would engage in fierce polemics against the Confucians.

Confucius was apparently a conservative; he worked to preserve tradition by teaching classical texts to students. Yet this act in itself can be seen as bold, if not revolutionary. He claimed that 'I transmit but do not innovate; and I believe in and love antiquity' (*Analects* 7.1). However, as Sima Qian (c. 145–86 BCE), one of the greatest Chinese historians and the author of *Shiji* (*The Records of the Grand Historian*), keenly observed, what Confucius did was to construct his own version of the historical records *Spring and Autumn Annals* (*Shiji*, Volume 48; Sima 1981: 228). More generally, what Confucius (and many of his followers) tried to do was conserve tradition by offering a new and often revolutionary interpretation if it.

The need for a new social glue

A key problem in the SAWS era was that the old social glue – li, rites, rituals and codes of conduct – had become political ineffective, both within the ruling class and between rulers and ruled, due to the expansion of states and the emergence of a society of strangers. Confucius seems to have wished to restore the Zhou li: 'The Zhou [li][5] was based upon those of the two previous dynasties, and was resplendent in culture. I am for the Zhou [li]' (*Analects* 3.14). However, discussion between him and his pupils on the ritual of three-year mourning – according to which one is required to abstain from holding political office, having luxuries, and enjoying entertainment for three years following the death of a parent – reveals that Confucius's conservatism does not equate to simple adherence to the past.

> Zai Wo [a pupil of Confucius] said [literally 'asked'], 'the three-year mourning period is too long. If the *junzi* stops practising li for three years, li will be in ruins... So one year is enough.
>   The master said, 'eating your rice [a delicacy at that time] and wearing your brocade [fine clothes], would you feel at ease?'
>   Zai Wo said, 'Yes I would.'
>   'If you feel at ease, then do it! The *junzi* in mourning finds no relish in good food, no pleasure in music, and no easy feeling in his home, which is why he does not do it. If you feel at ease, then do it!'
>   After Zai Wo left, the master said, 'How inhumane [not ren 仁] Zai Wo is![6] A child ceases to be nursed by his parents only after

he is 3 years old. Three years' mourning is observed throughout
the world.[7] Was Zai Wo not loved by his parents for three years?!'
(*Analects* 17.21)

A number of observations can be made on this passage. First, early
Confucians were concerned with li, as shown in Zai Wo's questioning
of a particular code of conduct, the three years' mourning. In spite
of his questioning this particular li, his concern seems to be also
rooted in preserving li. That is, the particular code of conduct, the
three-year mourning, may be detrimental to preserving li in general.
Second, Confucius does not answer Zai Wo's question by (merely)
remarking that this is how things are done according to the ancient
rules, as a straightforward conservative would say. Rather, he invokes
human emotion and moral sentiment, and offers a rational argument
on the basis of them. If one lacks these responses, one simply is
lacking in humanity. The focus for Confucius here is not whether
ancient codes of conduct will be broken; his concern, rather, is to
preserve the moral sentiments that form the foundation of humanity
(ren). Elsewhere Confucius asks, 'What can a man do with li if he is
not humane?' (*Analects* 3.3), implying that li (and its conservation)
is not fundamental whereas humanity is, and thus is the ultimate
foundation of li.

Thus, rather than seeking to conserve the li that served well as
the social glue in feudal society, Confucius holds up humanity as the
fundamental building block of a good society and its new social glue.
According to Confucius and other early Confucians, the reason that
we observe certain codes of social conduct is that we have certain
moral sentiments, such as filial love for our parents and parental
care for our children, along with compassion for others. External
practices (rites, rituals and social conduct) are expressions of our
internal moral sentiments. Mencius offers a very vivid and powerful
illustration of the moral sentiment of compassion:[8]

> The reason for me to say that all human beings have the heart that
> cannot bear [to see the sufferings of] others is this. If men suddenly

see a child about to fall into a well, they all have a feeling of alarm
and distress, not to gain friendship with the child's parents, nor to
seek the praise of their neighbours and friends, nor because they
dislike the cry of the child. From this we see that a man without the
feeling of compassion[9] is not a man... (*Mencius* 2A6)

What is worthy of note here? First, Mencius does not say that all
people automatically act according to their instinctive moral feelings.
Taking an action will depend upon a careful and assiduous cultivation
of moral sentiment. Second, some might argue that this instinctive
feeling of compassion is not as universal as the above story might lead
us to believe. For example, a child might not feel alarm and distress
in response to this situation. Here Mencius could say that this is not
because this child lacks compassion, but because he or she doesn't
understand the consequences of the other child's falling into a well.
What, then, of the sociopath, who understands the consequences
of a cruel act and, precisely because of this understanding, enjoys
it greatly? Mencius could argue that this person has the heart for
compassion, but it is covered up (lost) due to a lack of cultivation. But
if such a person never possessed this heart, Mencius would simply
say that they are not human. That is, for Mencius, 'human' is not
merely a biological but a moral concept. In other words, Mencius is
not merely describing how people are; the account he offers here is
intended to be normative. However, at the same time, his account
seems to apply to most (if not all) human beings descriptively. This
makes his normative account a good one. For it is realistic to a large
extent, but transcends the merely empirical, which makes his moral
philosophy a 'realistic utopia'[10] – a requirement, I think, for any
good moral philosophy.

Moreover, the term 'human being' for Mencius also has a clear
social dimension. What he says in a subsequent passage clearly reveals
this. According to an 'origin' story with a clear normative intention,
Mencius maintains that the government should first be responsible
for the physical well-being of its subjects. But when this objective
has been achieved, that is

[when the people] have a full belly and warm clothes on their
back, they almost degenerate to the level of brutes if they are
allowed to lead idle lives, without education and discipline. This
gave the sage King further cause for concern, and so he appointed
Xie as the Minister of Education whose duty was to teach the
people human relationships: love between father and son, duty
between ruler and subject, distinction between husband and wife,
precedence of the old over the young, and trust between friends.
(Mencius 3A4)

Thus, according to Mencius, it is these social or communal relationships, taught by the government, that make people human. A human
being in the biological sense, or as an individual entity, free of the
available social relationships, is not a human being. In other words,
the noble savage, the autonomous individual, for Mencius, is not
really a human being, but a human lookalike.

Therefore, for Mencius, it is the moral sentiment of compassion and social relations that make us human. In particular, this
moral sentiment is the slight (but fundamental) difference between
humans and beasts (Mencius 4B19). But it should be made clear that
this moral sentiment is different from conscience, if the latter is
understood as the innate quality, such as faith in a supreme being,
that can exist without necessarily involving other human beings, for
Mencius also emphasizes the social aspect of humanity. Indeed, from
both the common meaning of the term 'compassion' and Mencius'
story of the falling child, we can see that compassion is a feeling
for strangers. Now we can finally see how humanity, especially in
the form of compassion, was able to replace the old social glue that
could only be effective in a close-knit, small society. As observed,
the fundamental change in the SAWS period was the collapse of this
small-scale society, and the emergence of a large and populous state
without close bonds. Despite their apparent conservatism (respect for
the old rites and rituals), early Confucians anticipated the problem,
and tried to solve it by offering a new social glue suitable for this
emerging world.

A comparison may help illustrate this point further. It is curious to note that, in spite of the central status it enjoys in Mencius's and many Confucians' philosophy, compassion is not one of the four Greek cardinal virtues. Nor does it seem to be valued greatly by Ancient Romans, to judge by surviving historical and philosophical documents, in which praise for compassion is oddly lacking. It seems that the German philosopher Friedrich Nietzsche was correct when he claimed that pity or compassion was not valued as a virtue by the Ancient Greeks and Romans, but only made its appearance later in Western history (through Christianity). His diagnosis of this 'symptom' is as follows (see Nietzsche 1994, 2002). The Jews, who were enslaved by one group after another, were not happy with their status (being oppressed and looked down upon by the Romans), but were too weak to change it. They were also too bitter to accept their fate. So they revolted through conspiracy. That is, they wanted to invert the moral values of the nobles, rendering the weak (i.e. the Jews) the morally superior, and the strong (i.e. the Romans) the morally inferior. They tried to spread these new moral values – slave morality – in which, among other things, compassion (pity) became a virtue, in opposition to Ancient Greek and Roman values. According to Nietzsche, they succeeded in doing so through Jewish 'black arts' and by reinventing Judaism in the form of Christianity (Nietzsche 1994: 19–20).

However, this reading does not work at all in the Chinese context. Early Confucians were not an oppressed people. One might argue that they were like the old priests in Nietzsche's account, but, for Nietzsche, the slavish priestly morality could not be successfully spread without the conspiracy of a particular priestly and slavish people – the Jews. Thus, even if Nietzsche was correct in identifying the supposed 'symptom', his diagnosis was wide of the mark. Rather, the reason for compassion to become a virtue was the need to find a social glue for a large society of strangers. In the case of the Greek *polis* (city-state) and the early Roman republics, which were comparatively small, friendship served as an effective social glue. In contrast, the Hellenistic period and that of the later Roman empire, when society became large and complicated, moral philosophies that emphasized compassion duly emerged. However, this trend slowed down with the establishment of the feudal system, which, through its pyramid-like hierarchy, divided a relatively large society into small communities. When this hierarchy collapsed during Western modernization, compassion (along with other values such as equality) finally became a dominant virtue. It would subsequently be celebrated by many modern European thinkers, and cause Nietzsche, a Classicist by training and an aficionado of Roman culture, to suffer distress and despair.

The cultivation of humanity:
expanding circles and a universal yet unequal love

How do we cultivate compassion or humanity? Confucius's answer is 'to take as analogy what is near at hand' (*Analects* 6.30). What is commonly near at hand is one's own self and family. In the *Mencius*, a king confesses that he has weaknesses (literally 'illnesses'): a fondness for money and for beautiful women. In his response to this concern of the king, Mencius declares that these predilections are important in that they can help a king understand that his people must have the same desires as he does; if this understanding leads him to be mindful of his people's needs, he will become a good king (*Mencius* 1B5). This account offers an interesting contrast to an example given by Immanuel Kant of how an action can have moral worth. Kant claims that if a man is overshadowed by his own grief to the extent that it extinguishes his sympathy for the fate of others, or if by nature he is cold and indifferent to others' sufferings, then the philanthropic action that he takes possesses 'genuine moral worth' (Kant 1998: 12–13; 4:398–399).

Understanding one's own needs is merely a necessary condition for taking care of those of others. We require a strong moral sense of compassion to motivate us to act for others. Compassion leads us outward, expanding our self-love towards others. A notable place to cultivate compassion is the family. For, on the one hand, most people feel bound to and have a loving feeling for their family, almost commensurate with one's self-love. On the other hand, caring for family members is also the first step beyond one's mere self and self-love, inasmuch as it is reaching out to others. This may have been the reason that, when Confucius and Mencius talk about humanity, they tend to emphasize two things: filial love (see the discussion, above, between Confucius and his pupils on three years' mourning) and compassion (see Mencius's story of the falling child). For they are deeply interconnected. It is also perhaps why Confucians pay so much attention to filial love. Many misunderstand this as an unreflective and thus unphilosophical expression of familialism – that is, placing family interests above all else – which seems a natural response and one still prevalent, especially in many rural societies, where the family constitutes the stable unit of community. Whereas in fact, for Confucians, filial love is important because it is the most natural stepping stone enabling human beings to expand their care outwards. This rationale is stated explicitly in the *Analects*:

> It is a rare thing for someone who is filial to his parents and respectful to his older brothers to defy superiors. And it is unheard of for those who do not defy superiors to be keen on initiating rebellion. Exemplary persons [junzi] concentrate their efforts on the root, for the root having taken hold, the Way will grow therefrom. Being filial to one's parents and being respectful to one's older brothers is the root of humanity! (1.2)

Clearly, this passage suggests that communal and political relations are analogous to and should be modelled on familial relations. We need to start from family relations and expand such familial care outwardly. As Mencius puts it,

> Treat the elderly of my own family [as they should be treated], and extend this treatment to the elderly of other families; treat the young of my own family [as they should be treated], and

extend this to the young of other families.... Thus extending one's humanity outwards can protect everyone within the Four Seas [held to be the boundaries of the world], and not extending one's humanity cannot even protect one's wife and sons. (*Mencius* 1A7)

If one keeps extending one's care, eventually one will embrace everything in the universe. This ideal is beautifully illustrated by a later Confucian thinker, Zhang Zai 張載 (1020–1077), in his famous 'Western Inscription':

Heaven [qian 乾] is called my father and Earth [kun 坤] is called my mother. And I, this tiny thing, find an intimate place in their midst.

Hence, what fills Heaven and Earth is my body, and what directs Heaven and Earth is my nature. All people are my siblings, and all living things are my companions. The great ruler is the eldest son of my parents, and his ministers are his retainers. To respect those great in years is the way to 'treat the elderly as the elderly should be treated'. To be loving to the orphaned and the weak is the way to 'treat the young as the young should be treated.' ... All in the world who are tired, infirm, crippled or sick; brotherless, childless, widows or widowers – they are all my siblings who are helpless and have no one else to appeal to....

Riches, honour, good fortune and abundance shall enrich my life, while poverty, a humble station, care and sorrow shall discipline me to fulfilment. In life I follow and serve [Heaven and Earth], and in death I shall be at peace.[11]

We can see from this passage that the ideal of universal love is both ethical and political; it is good for the world and brings great peace to oneself.

Confucian moral cultivation is like concentric circles that start from the self and family, and move outwardly until they embrace the whole world. This clearly serves as an inspiring ideal; it is unlikely to be achieved by any real human being.

Moreover, it should be noted that, for Mencius, it is also natural and justified for everyone, including a person capable of universal love (should there be such a person), to care more about those with whom he or she has closer bonds – for instance, trying to save a drowning mother before helping anyone else. This is the Confucian idea of graded love (爱有差等). This tenet is also intended to contrast the Confucian stance with that of the Mohist. (Mohism, as we have seen, was a dominant school of thought during the SAWS, especially in the Warring States period, which is why for Mencius and other thinkers it was a serious target; however, its influence on the political stage all but disappeared after the Qin dynasty, the reason for which is a hotly debated issue.) Mohism was said – by Mencius, for example – to embrace universal love without discrimination or distinction. For Mencius, this position 'amounts to a denial of one's father' (*Mencius* 3B9). Confucian love is universal and unequal or hierarchical at the same time. Wang Yangming 王阳明 (1472–1528), one of the most important later Confucians, who was greatly influenced by Mencius, illustrated this love nicely. According to *Record of Instructions* 传习录,

> Someone asked, 'A great man and an object are one, but why does *The Great Learning* also say that something is favoured [hou 厚, literally 'thick'] and something is not [bo 薄, literally 'thin']?' The master [Wang Yangming] said, 'in principle, there are naturally some things favoured and some things not. For example, the body is one, but [when there is a danger] the hands and feet are used to protect the head and face. Does this mean that the hands and feet are not favoured? This is how it should be. We love both beasts and plants, but the heart can bear to use plants to feed beasts. We love both human beings and beasts, but the heart can bear to slaughter beasts to feed family, to make sacrifices and to treat guests. We love both our closest kin and people in the street. But if there is very little food and soup, one survives if one gets it and dies if one does not, and if there is not enough food to save two, the heart can bear to save the closest kin and not the person in the street. This is how it should be. When it is between my body and the closest kin, we can no longer make the distinction. For to treat people humanely and to treat things lovingly come from this [love of one's own body and closest kin]. If one can bear [to do anything] here, one can bear [to do anything] anywhere. (Wang 1992: 108, my translation)

To sum up, the new social glue discovered or invented by early Confucians was ren, humanity. An important aspect of humanity is compassion, which serves to bind together a large and populous society of strangers. To cultivate this moral sentiment, we start from filial love and expand outwards. The ideal is universal but unequal love. With this understanding, let us consider some further implications.

Confucianism, familialism and relations between the private and the public

Confucianism is often blamed for the spreading of corruption in both traditional and contemporary China. For it is described as a teaching that promotes amoral familialism (embodied by Godfather Don Corleone's motto 'never go against your family') and cronyism. One passage that is often mentioned is *Analects* 13.18. The governor of She tells Confucius that an upright man in his village bore witness against his father, who took a sheep on the sly. Confucius's response is that in his village uprightness lies in mutual concealment between father and son. This is an example of the Confucian idea of mutual concealment among kin. But we need to consider carefully the message of this story. First, we note that what is concealed is misconduct (stealing a sheep), not a serious crime like murder. Second, and more importantly, the hidden rationale in this case is not that obeying the law is not important, compared to protecting one's family. Rather, from a Confucian point of view, the message is that without loving relations among members of society, the demand to obey laws will become oppressive and the society will disintegrate.[12] Let us do a thought experiment here. If the son turns his father in, the father will be jailed. The father will thus stop trusting his son, the person whom he is supposed to trust the most. With his trust in others undermined, is it realistic to expect this petty criminal to be rehabilitated? In contrast, to conceal the father's petty crime, for a Confucian, does not mean letting him go free. Rather, by concealing the father's misconduct, thus preserving the loving relationship and trust, one can then more effectively help him right his wrongs.[13]

It should by now be clear that to suggest that the Confucian idea of graded love promotes cronyism would be to demonstrate a basic misunderstanding of Confucianism. For central to the Confucian credo is the necessity to extend one's love; failure to do so, as Mencius tells us, means one cannot even protect one's own family (*Mencius* 1A7). The above misunderstanding is so obvious that even to criticize it seems facile. Nevertheless, the point must be made because the misconception remains widespread among both Westerners (due to their superficial understanding of Chinese philosophy) and Chinese (the consequence of over a hundred years of fierce but misguided criticism of tradition).

In fact, not only was Confucianism not meant to promote familialism and cronyism, it was actually meant to cure it. As was mentioned, SAWS was an era in which the old order was collapsing, or simply an orderless era. Small cliques were formed, which fought for their private interests to the detriment of the public good. Early Confucians were keenly aware of the problems. A focus common to the *Analects*, the *Mencius* and the *Xun Zi* is how to restore order, and of crucial concern is how to resolve the conflict between private and public. This, of course, is a universal political problem, one that has preoccupied political thinkers of all ages and locales. For example, notwithstanding the many differences between a Greek city-state and a SAWS-era state, Plato's *Republic* is centrally concerned with the private–public conflict. The solution offered there is to suppress the private (or at least those aspects of the private held to be in conflict with the public interest) completely, including abolishing the traditional family in favour of conceiving the entire city-state as a big family with no factions. Many modern Western thinkers, in contrast, worry about public interference with the private realm, and try to find ways to protect the private by drawing a sharp line between the two. Of course, different people focus on different aspects of the private. For example, in America, conservatives often try to keep the government's hand out of citizens' pockets, while at the same time – in the case of moral conservatives – wanting it to get into people's bedrooms; whereas liberals, on the other hand, strive to keep the government's hand out of people's bedrooms, while urging it to dip into people's pockets.

In spite of their different foci, both the *Republic* and many modern Western thinkers concentrate almost exclusively on conflicting aspects between the private and the public. Early Confucians also saw these, but they understood that the division between the two realms is not sharp, and that aspects of the private can be constructive in relation to the public interest. In particular, the family belongs to the private realm if we compare it to the community, but it belongs to the public realm when held against the mere self. Thus, to cultivate familial relations does not necessarily lead to the dominance of private interests over public. With this fundamental insight, the early Confucians' solution to the conflict between the private and the public was not to suppress the private completely, but to cultivate its constructive aspects so as to overcome the ones in conflict with the public. The remedy for familialism is not abolition of the family, as the *Republic* appears to suggest, but cultivation of familial care, thereby extending the familial boundary and turning familial care into fully fledged compassion.

It is interesting to note that the apparent ideal in the *Republic* is to make the whole city-state a big family by, paradoxically, abolishing the traditional family; in this big family, everyone is 'a brother, or a sister, or a father, or a mother, or a son, or a daughter or their descendants or ancestors' (*Republic* 463c; Bloom 1991: 143). But it is in China that this ideal has been realized. A sense of community and the perception of the state as a big family are deep in the Chinese psyche, due in large part to Confucian thought. The contemporary Chinese term for 'state', *guojia* 国家, means literally 'state-family'. The Chinese term for 'all', *dajia* 大家, means literally 'the big family'. A stranger is often introduced as 'uncle Li', 'aunt Zhou', 'sister Zhao', or 'brother Bai', and so on. What was a wild dream in the *Republic* has, to an extent, become a reality in China. Importantly, Confucians would say that it is a pipe dream to make the state a big family while abolishing the traditional family. For to make the state a big family is to take advantage of the close ties of familial relations. Without natural families, these ties could not be cultivated, and terms such as 'brother' and 'sister' would lose their meaning. The *Republic*, then, appears to want to have its cake and to eat it. In the Cultural Revolution in China, Mao Zedong and his followers also tried to achieve exactly this pipe dream, by abolishing the traditional family in favour of the collective.

Regarding modern and contemporary Westerners' concern with protecting the private, Confucians have two reservations. The first is that the rationale for protecting the private comes from the origin myth peculiar to modern Western philosophy: that we were once all free and autonomous individuals. But there were disadvantages for us in that free but lonely world. So we agreed to form a society by giving up some of our autonomy. But there are aspects that we would never give up; and so when the state fails to deliver the service that attracts us to it, we can reclaim our original autonomy. As we have seen, the early Confucians simply did not buy this story. For them, human beings are social to the core. This means not that we should therefore abolish rights but that we should defend rights and democracy not simply by claiming for them a sacred status but by referring them to some higher good. For example, Confucians can defend freedom of speech. But they would not say that this freedom is sacred, or that government has no right to interfere with people's verbal and written expression. Instead they may say that freedom of speech is instrumental to good policymaking and should thus be protected.

The second reservation concerns modern Western thinkers' idea of protecting the private realm by presupposing a sharp boundary between private and public, something the Confucian continuous and complementary model (no sharp division between the private and the public, and the relation between the two realms is not purely one of conflict) denies. The modern Western tenet that certain choices are for an individual to make and the state should stay out of them presupposes that these choices are strictly private and will not cause harm to others. But if the distinction between the private and the public is in fact relative, and we are all interconnected with each other, then the above presupposition becomes highly questionable. Again, this does not mean that we should no longer protect the private realm; it simply suggests that this protection cannot be provided as straightforwardly as many believe.

Confucianism versus the nation-state

Confucians discover humanity as the new social glue for a large state, and try to find a middle ground between the unabashed celebration of self-interest and the negation of the private. These ideas have implications for another key issue in China's early modernity, that of international relations (including just war, international aid, etc.). State relations during the SAWS resemble in many ways state relations during Western modernization. The Zhou king ceased being a supranational authority, and states became independent entities with their own interests. Similar processes occurred in post-Westphalian Europe. But there is one crucial difference. What emerged in Europe was nation-states based mostly on nationality,[14] whereas people of different states during the SAWS still held to the view that there was a close cultural connection among them all. This belief was developed by early Confucians into a normative account of national identity.

According to this account, what makes someone Chinese is culture, and not ethnicity in the sense of perceived blood relationship. For Confucians, the core of this culture comes from the classical works of the past and the spirit of humanity underlying them. A passage from the Mencius beautifully illustrates this understanding (3A4). Mencius praises Chen Liang, a native of the state of Chu, a state that the Chinese looked down upon as almost barbarous and not as a bona fide Xia (Chinese) state. He points out that, in spite of his 'barbaric' origin, Chen Liang managed to grasp Chinese culture (in the form of the teachings of Confucius) better than the scholars from the Chinese states. In contrast, some of his disciples, although likely from a *Xia* state, failed to conform to Chinese culture and thus degraded themselves to the level of barbarians. This passage clearly implies that 'Chinese-ness' depends not upon a person's state of birth or ethnic nationality, but on mastery of Chinese culture – the kind of culture that early Confucians sanctioned.

In contrast to ethnicity-based nationality, this culture-based state identity is inclusive, because whereas one can't change one's ethnicity in order to become a member of a nation-state, one can change one's cultural identity to become a member of a state whose basis is culture. One might object by arguing that conversion can be as problematic as changing one's ethnicity. To appreciate this point, one need only think about religious killings in European history. But the kind of culture advocated by early Confucians to serve as the foundation of state identity is much thinner than religion, and one can adopt both a 'non-Chinese' religion and the cultural identity. One interesting example concerns the Jewish diaspora. Historically Jews have been persecuted all over the world, but the only known case of peaceful assimilation occurred in China, where, having settled for reasons of commerce, they willingly adopted the Chinese way of life while maintaining their faith for a considerable time.[15] Generally speaking, it is possible (as both the past and the present testify) to be a Confucian Muslim, a Confucian Christian or a Confucian Jew. In contrast, no one can be an Islamic Christian or a Catholic Methodist.

The Confucian understanding of cultural identity and its prevalence in Chinese history are one reason that, although historically the Chinese were defeated, even conquered, by 'barbaric' nomads, their culture has lasted, making China the country with the longest continuous state identity. The conquerors in the past were either assimilated into Chinese culture, and thus became Chinese themselves, or were eventually driven out due to their failure to assimilate. To be clear, Chinese dynasties were at times imperialistic or expansionistic; however, this expansion was effected through a slow cultural assimilation rather than mere military dominance over 'aliens' (people with different cultures). That is, they transformed peoples into Chinese and rendered their land Chinese not simply by killing or oppressing them, in the manner of many Western nation-states and empires, but by 'converting' them through the soft power of a purportedly superior culture.[16] This expansion was slow because of the need to maintain cultural homogeneity, but when it was achieved it was founded on solid ground and was thus able to last longer than if government had been imposed. By contrast, Western colonial empires often consisted of an alien central government imposing rules on an empire of diverse cultures and identities. It is small wonder that when this imperial government collapsed, the empire dissolved. An alternative was to kill off the indigenous residents, as in the case of white Americans exterminating American natives. By contrast, the Chinese version of soft cultural competition was better than brute conquest and political oppression inasmuch as it didn't advocate eliminating a culture by force, but rather encouraged competition among cultures. This model can lead a culture to better itself and thus produce a flourishing of diverse cultures, in contrast to direct oppression, on the one hand, and unprincipled tolerance, on the other.

Moreover, the exclusivity of the nation-state is also embodied in the sharp distinction drawn between friends and enemies. People of a nation or within the borders of a nation all belong together, and their interests are the highest good ('my country, right or wrong'). There is little regard for peoples of other nations, and realpolitik is the only way to go. But for Confucians, although it is natural and justified to put ones one's compatriots' interests above those of others, one should not thereby practise realpolitik, giving no regard to the suffering of aliens. For humanity is the ultimate good, necessitating humane treatment of each and every human being. To behave otherwise would mean we had ceased to be human ourselves, because by treating other humans inhumanely we sacrifice our own humanity. An alternative to the realpolitik that characterizes contemporary

Western political thought is cosmopolitanism, advocating universal and equal love. But, as we have seen, Confucians would say this is too idealistic, paying insufficient attention to humans' natural and justifiable sentiments. Hence, instead of people loving everyone equally, cosmopolitanism may lead them to love no one. Thus, for Confucians, realpolitik is too cruel and cosmopolitanism is too naive. In contrast, the application to international relations of the Confucian idea of universal but hierarchical love offers a realistic utopia for the global community.

There are, however, some problems with the Confucian model. On the one hand, although the kind of culture that serves as the identity of the state is rather thin, it can still be too thick in comparison with the alternatives. Part of the national identity of the contemporary USA is also culture, but it is even thinner and thus more inclusive than the Confucian model. For example, a difficult issue for China now, both practically and theoretically, is how to absorb Tibetans and Uyghurs fully into the Chinese state (which may not embrace the thin cultural identity Confucians propose), an issue that wouldn't be a theoretical problem for the American model.[17] On the other hand, it might be considered that the Confucian cultural identity is too thin. Culture as Confucians understand it can be shared by two states, which might raise the question of why they should remain independent from each other. For Confucians, the maintenance of borders between states is of no great concern. On this note, let us turn to another subject in the early Confucian theory of international relations: just war and international peace.

The Confucian theory of just war and international peace

The collapse of feudalism and overlordship (through the office of the Zhou king) led to the emergence of independent states, which then began warring against each other. Thus, a key issue of China's early modernity was how to deal with the issue of wars and how to achieve international peace. Early Confucians addressed the issue with their notion of humanity and the idea of culture-based identity. For them, the only justifiable basis for any war (as well as peace) is humanity. They objected to wars waged merely for the sake of conquest and domination or in pursuit of naked national interest. To wage a just war against another state presupposes that the people of the other state are suffering under bad rule (bad in the sense that these people's basic spiritual and physical needs cannot be satisfied due to the failure of their ruler); hence a war of liberation is the only kind of justifiable non-defensive war.

Early Confucians urged caution against wars, including those waged for purportedly humanitarian reasons. In spite of their ideals, early Confucians had an understanding of the limit of humans. There are situations in which even sages can do little to make a difference (although we still need to do our best regardless). This is perhaps one reason that Confucians lack missionary zeal. More importantly, even if people of another state are actually suffering, it may take time for them to realize it and be ready for change. Otherwise, the consequence might be an unnecessary loss of life and perhaps even the flocking of suffering people to support bad rulers. The principle that suffering people have to be ready to act for themselves is reflected, for example, in the firm belief of the *Mencius* that every human has the capacity to be enlightened, but that this has to achieved by himself or herself willingly. An example is the tale of a stupid and impatient farmer who wishes to help his seedlings grow by pulling them up, but of course simply succeeds in killing them (*Mencius* 2A2).

Reference to the *Analects* and the *Mencius* may help to illustrate further the Confucian stance on war. In a conversation (*Analects* 16.1), two of Confucius's pupils who served Lord Ji, a powerful lord in the state of Lu, are plotting with Lord Ji to attack another lord, the lord of Zhuanyu. Confucius points out that the lord of Zhuanyu and his fief had been a bulwark of the state, and that the lord had not done anything wrong. But one of his pupils points out that this fief is close to one of his lord's fiefs (the fief of Bei 費), and it is strongly fortified, which is why he and his lord wish to destroy it. Confucius then points out that the stability of the state or a fief depends on it treating its own people well. If people of one's own state are treated well, but people from a different state or fief remain intractable and even pose a potential threat, we should strive to improve our civilization and moral character in order to win them over. Finally, Confucius pointedly observes that the threat to the fief of Lord Ji does not really come from outside; rather, it comes from within – that is, from Lord Ji's lack of humanity and his practice of realpolitik. In fact, Lord Ji was one of three powerful ministers who usurped the power of the throne, notwithstanding the nominal homage paid to the ruler of Lu. An interesting twist to this story is that in the next chapter of the *Analects* (17.5), the fief of Bei, which is said to be threatened by the other lord's fief, uses its power and strong fortification to rebel against Lord Ji. Small wonder, perhaps, in light of the moral example Lord Ji set his subjects, as Confucius suggests in his observation that the real threat to Lord Ji came from within. The general message from this passage is that war should be our last resort: the best way to disarm a threat and prevail in the world is to become a moral exemplar. On account of this Confucian understanding, rulers of traditional Chinese states who were keen on waging war – albeit ostensibly in the best interests of the people – were rarely praised, and were often criticized.

A passage in the *Mencius* (1A5) further shows the crucial role humanity plays in the strength of a state. King Hui of the state of Wei, one of the seven strong states during the Warring States period, bemoans the fact that his state, though once the strongest, was under his rule repeatedly defeated by other strong states. He thus asks Mencius how to make his state strong. Mencius answers:

> A territory which is only 100 li by 100 li [a unit of distance, perhaps around half a kilometre, in Mencius's time] is sufficient for its ruler to become a true king [ruling over all states]. If Your Majesty will practise humane governance to the people – sparing

in the use of punishments and fines, and making the taxes and levies light, so that the fields shall be ploughed deep and the weeds shall be removed in time, and that the strong-bodied, during their days of leisure, shall cultivate their filial piety, fraternal respectfulness, loyalty and trustworthiness, serving thereby, at home, their fathers and elder brothers, and, outside home, their elders and superiors – then you can make these people who are armed with nothing but staves inflict defeat on the armies of Qin and Chu [two powerful states at the time], who are armed with strong armour and sharp weapons. [For] the rulers of those states rob their people of their time [during the farming season], so that they cannot plough and weed their fields to support their parents. Their parents suffer from cold and hunger, and their brothers, wives and children are separated and scattered. Those rulers push their people into pits and into water. If Your Majesty should move to punish them, who will be there to oppose you? Hence it is said, 'The man of humanity has no match.' I beg of you not to have any more doubts. (Mencius 1A5)

In a later passage, Mencius insists: 'If he tends his people, no one and nothing can stop him from becoming a true king' (Mencius 1A7).

The message of these passages is clear, although it might be considered by some to be over-optimistic. For it is claimed that the people from a state with a humane ruler can defeat other inhumane states even if the former have far inferior weaponry than the latter. It is also claimed that even a small state (i.e. one with a territory of 100 li by 100 li) can unify all other states if it practises humanity. Anyone with knowledge of human history or with a realistic perspective may find these claims naive and even ridiculous. After all, Mencius, who knew of the brutal wars and conquests during the SAWS, should know better. However, if we take a closer look at Mencius's claims, we may detect a subtler message. The interlocutors in Mencius 1A5 and 1A7 are the kings of two of the largest, most powerful and technologically advanced states during the Warring States period. It may be the case that the claims for the power of humanity are meant to inspire, and should not be taken at face value. Indeed, when talking to Duke Wen of Teng, a very small state, Mencius reveals his realistic side (Mencius

1B13, 1B14, 1B15). Duke Wen asks Mencius how to defend his state, and Mencius basically offers two options. The first option is to beef up the defences by digging deeper moats and building higher walls; the state might then be saved if the people are prepared to die rather than desert the state. The second option is for the duke to abandon his land and move to a safer place; if his people follow him, they can start over again from there. Then, if future rulers of this state keep practising humane government in the new land, eventually a ruler will become the true king (one who is able to make the state invincible and to spread humanity to the whole world) – although Mencius seems hesitant, as he avers that success also depends upon fortune. Thus Mencius did not really believe that a state based on humane rule can achieve security and prosperity no matter what. However, if a state cannot save itself during a turbulent time, governing humanely offers the only chance for survival. Should this fail, the state and its people can comfort themselves with the fact that they die as a state of humans, not a state of ruthless beasts.

When it is humane and strong, a state may need to engage in a war of liberation. Mencius also offered clear criteria for this kind of war. It should be noted in the long passage quoted above that Mencius claims that the two other strong states treated their subjects badly, but he doesn't back up this claim with any historical evidence. We should infer from this that Mencius is not talking about historical reality, but implicitly offering criteria for an offensive war. He makes the criteria more explicit in other passages. For example, the state of Qi attacked and defeated the State of Yan (these being two of the seven strongest states at the time), and King Xuan of Qi asks Mencius if his state should annex Yan. Mencius answers:

> If the people of Yen will be pleased with the annexation, then do so... If the people of Yen will not be pleased with the annexation, then do not do so... When, with the strength of your state of ten thousand chariots, you attacked another state of ten thousand chariots, and the people brought baskets of rice and bottles of drink to meet Your Majesty's army,[18] was there any other reason

for this but that they hoped to escape from fire and water? Should the water become deeper and the fire hotter, they would have no alternative but to turn elsewhere [to be saved]. (*Mencius* 1B10)

The message of this passage is clear: for an offensive war to be justified, the people attacked have to welcome the attack. If the winner fails to deliver what was promised, it is justified for it to be driven out. We can see from this that even a defensive war is not necessarily justified if the state being defended is inhumane.

To cite a contemporary example, some argued that the second US attack on Iraq was justifiable in the name of liberating Iraqis from the brutal rule of Saddam Hussein. Some even predicted that the Iraqis would welcome the American army on the streets. If the welcome had been long-lasting, it would have provided justification for a 'pre-emptive' war that Confucians could accept.[19] But since this prediction failed to materialize, the Iraq war was not just from a Confucian point of view.

In another passage, it is said that Earl Ge, the ruler of the state adjacent to Tang's state (Tang being the humane ruler who founded the Shang dynasty), was a bad ruler. Tang offered aid to him, but Earl Ge squandered it. He even robbed and killed a small boy who, at the urging of Tang, offered help. King Tang then attacked the state of Ge. Mencius tells us:

When King Tang marched on the east, the western barbarians complained; he marched on the south, the northern barbarians complained. They said, 'Why does he not come to us first?'[20] The people longed for his coming, as they longed for rain during a severe drought... *The Book of Documents* says, 'We are waiting for our king. When he comes, there won't be sufferings anymore!'[21] (*Mencius* 3B5)

Thus a purported war of liberation is truly a war of liberation when the people attacked and liberated complain only about being attacked late. To hope for such an expression of approval may appear to be overly idealistic. Yet this complaint may well have been expressed by peoples of the states who were liberated late in World War II by the American and British armies.

On the subject of wars waged merely for the sake of conquest, Mencius simply asserts, without much elaboration, that it is possible for an inhumane state to conquer another state, but it is not possible for an inhumane state to conquer the world (*Mencius* 7B13).

Implications of Confucian ideas for environmentalism, animal rights and feminism

The Confucian ideas of humanity, universal and unequal love, and relations between the private and the public, can also shed new light on contemporary issues. For example, on the environment, unfortunately human beings are often caught in a dilemma between its protection and enjoying a reasonably good life. Even worse, those in developing countries appear to be faced with the following choice: either damage the environment to survive, or save the environment and starve to death. In their call for protection of the environment, some radical environmentalists fail to address people's desire for a good life (be it materially comfortable or spiritually satisfying). They either believe that the environment is sacred or pin their hopes on turning people into 'noble savages', as in the idealized Native American tribes in the movie *Dances with Wolves*. Even worse, there is a running complaint from developed countries about the pollution generated by China, India and other developing countries, the reason for which is straightforwardly that people wish for the comfortable lifestyle enjoyed by developed countries, and that involves producing the multitude of material goods demanded by developed countries, and its corollary, pollution! And yet, the stance of the other extreme (to satisfy human needs with no regard to the environment), which is opposite to the above stance that we should save the environment even at the cost of the survival and a reasonably good life of (certain) human beings, seems to be equally problematic.

On this issue, Confucians offer an alternative to the two extremes. In the Confucian hierarchy of love, human flourishing is clearly higher than the good of the environment; furthermore there is nothing wrong with people wanting to have some luxuries in life. But this does not mean that we should pay no heed to the effects we have on the environment. First, our descendants' survival depends on the environment; we cannot squander its resources, leaving our descendants nothing. This concern finds support in Confucians' emphasis on the social nature of human existence. As shown in the passage quoted from the *Mencius* 3A4, we would not be human if all we managed was to fill our own bellies – that is, if we only satisfy our physical needs. Rather, we are human because we participate in certain social relations. This non-individualistic understanding of human existence may guide us more readily to a long-term consideration of the effects of human activity on the environment than an individualist approach.

Second, for Confucians human needs are the priority, but these must include non-physical wants as well. To live in an air-conditioned mansion at the price of a dirtier and uglier world does not truly satisfy our needs, for we, as human beings, wish to live in a beautiful world (and in an air-conditioned house if possible). Acknowledgement of the complexity of human needs and of the effort required to address them makes Confucianism better equipped to deal with environmental issues than doctrines focused upon a single value.

Third, the Confucian principle that care for human beings comes first does not mean that we should have no care for the environment. As beautifully illustrated in Zhang Zai's 'Western Inscription' (cited above), everything in the world is a friend of mine, and a part of me. There is an almost mystical oneness of everything in the world. The Confucian model of concentric circles, though hierarchical, is all-inclusive as an ideal.

The last two points are well illustrated by anecdotes about Zhou Dunyi 周敦颐 (1017–1073) and Cheng Yi 程颐 (1033–1107), two later Confucians and leading voices of the Neo-Confucian movement.

It was recorded that Zhou refused to cut the grass in front of his windows. When asked why he did this, he said '[it is] as if [it] were my own family' (Cheng and Cheng 1992, Vol. 3: 54).[22] Cheng, when employed as the emperor's private tutor, saw him playfully break a twig of a weeping willow tree. He remarked to the emperor, '[the tree] was being reborn and growing in early spring, and [you] shouldn't break [a twig from it] and damage [it] for no reason' (Cheng and Cheng 1992: Appendix, 266).

It can therefore be argued that the Confucian position on the environment offers a sympathetic ear to those caught in the dilemma between survival and environmental needs. Being mindful of humans' natural tendency to think about what is 'near' and prioritize their concerns accordingly, Confucianism may be able to nudge people into thinking more productively of values beyond mere material self-interest. Such transcendence of the material self is not so much the negation of the self as the fulfilment of it. Thus, Confucians would say that this informed approach offers a better way to deal with complex environmental issues, and its sympathetic stance will appeal to people more than the aforementioned extreme positions.

By a similar rationale, we can see how Confucians might address the contemporary issue of animal rights.[23] Clearly, 'rights' may well be a concept alien to Confucian thinking, because they pay much attention to obligations or duties. But when thinking about animals, it may seem a little strange to speak of their rights. For example, in what sense does a tiger have a right to live? Does it consider our right to live when it attacks and eats human beings? In this scenario, Confucian talk of obligations sounds more natural. As human beings, we have compassion; this compassion is extendable to animals and even to all objects in the world. Thus, if we deserve to be called human beings, we should show care and obligation to animals. It is true that the basis for the humane treatment of animals is different (obligations as opposed to rights), but the Confucian understanding and discourse of rights can have a degree of overlapping consensus, and it may be this that is most important.

As another example, let us consider why we should save a whale that is stuck somewhere, given that the resources we spend on doing so could save a few starving babies in Africa. Simply asserting that both the whale and human babies have the right to live doesn't address the issue, which is really about the ranking of rights. Confucian teachings, however, clearly put human needs above those of animals. However, this doesn't mean that Confucians would support, for example, the killing of sharks on the grounds that shark fins are considered a delicacy by some human beings. As with the environmental issue, for Confucians the fact that human needs come first doesn't justify the neglect of animals' needs; indeed, caring for animals is itself also a human need (it is what makes us human; a rich animal world is an element of a good human life). In short, although Confucianism is clearly human-centric and obligation-oriented, it can endorse practices supported by animal rights campaigners and offer a more nuanced understanding of the ranking of complex human concerns than a singular focus on either animal welfare or narrowly defined human needs.

Let us consider some passages from early Confucian texts to help us understand their position on the care and humane treatment of animals. In the *Analects* (7.27), it is said that Confucius when fishing 'used a fishing line but not a cable [to which a number of fishing lines are attached],' and when hunting he 'did not shoot at roosting birds'. It is recorded elsewhere that, though poor, Confucius tried to save the curtains and covers of his carriage to wrap the corpses of his horse and dog when burying them (Wang 1991: ch. 43, 121; *Tangong Xia* 檀弓下 chapter of the *Classic of Rites* or *Liji* 礼记).

In the *Mencius*, a reason is offered for the humane treatment of animals. In *Mencius* 1A7, King Xuan of Qi sees that an ox is about to be killed for some ceremonial ritual, and says to the person leading the ox, 'Spare it. I cannot bear to see it shrinking with fear, like an innocent man going to the place of execution.' Abandoning the ceremony is considered to be out of the question, and so he orders the sacrifice of a lamb instead. But since lambs had less value than oxen, they were not considered as great a sacrifice as oxen (Jiao 1986: 48–50), and thus the king was suspected by the people of begrudging the expense, which the king vehemently denied. Mencius explains why the people have this suspicion:

> You must not be surprised that the people thought that you were miserly. You used a small animal in place of a big one. How were they to know? If you were pained by the animal going innocently to its death, what was there to choose between an ox and a lamb?

After the king denies one more time that he was motivated by monetary concerns, Mencius explains what could be behind the king's action:

> It is the way of a humane man. You saw the ox but not the lamb. The attitude of a gentleman towards animals is this: once having seen them alive, he cannot bear to see them die, and once having heard their cry, he cannot bear to eat their flesh. That is why the gentleman keeps his distance from the kitchen.

The last line of this quotation is from the Confucian classic Liji (Volume 6, ch. 13), a book about the proper conduct of gentlemen. Mencius here offers a Confucian interpretation of this code of conduct, as Confucius did for the principle of three years' mourning.

It is time to clarify a number of points.[24] In spite of the different theoretical foundations, the Confucian principle of care for animals may lead to practices similar to those called for by animal rights campaigners. For example, Confucians would be against cruelty to animals, in favour of humane animal husbandry, and so on. It is true that Confucian care is based upon a hierarchy centred on human beings. Yet people may find this more sensible than a view based upon the sanctity of animal rights. If we take the latter view, there seems to be no basis for us to treat our pets better than wild animals, or to treat animals that look more like humans (such as chimps) better than animals that look less so (such as cockroaches), both of which may be considered natural responses. But for the Confucian, these differential treatments are justified. In fact, the

Confucian stance might even broaden the scope of our caring and offer a reasonable ranking when the field is broadened. Why do we care about the well-being of animals while disregarding that of plants? Should we develop plant rights? How should we prioritize between animal rights and plant rights? From a few passages quoted in this chapter, we can determine that Confucian care does indeed extend to plants, although it is reasonable to rank their well-being below that of animals. In fact, Confucian care can even be extended to inanimate objects. For example, as one might expect, early Confucians were against using live people as funerary sacrifices. According to Mencius, Confucius went a step further, stating that 'The inventor of burial figures in human form deserves not to have any progeny' (*Mencius* 1A4). After all, care for other animate and inanimate objects comes from human compassion, as exemplified by the king's reaction to the imagined killing of the ox ('like an innocent man going to the place of execution'). By extension, Confucians would find it objectionable for someone to enjoy the virtual killing involved in some computer games.

The Confucian understanding of humanity and of relations between the private and the public can also make a contribution to the issue of equality between men and women in politics. Clearly, early Confucians were not feminists and didn't speak highly of women, but nor did most thinkers until quite recently. The most important issue, when considering the Confucian attitude towards women and how it might see the (recently emerged) issue of equality between men and women, is whether the negative opinion of women is rooted in the Confucian philosophical system itself or is merely a reflection of the customary views of the times. I lean towards the latter view. In fact, the early Confucian view of humanity and of the relations between the private and the public, which I consider to be an integral part of Confucian political philosophy, may offer some support to the cause of gender equality in politics. To follow up this claim, let us examine what some might argue is the first 'feminist' account in human history.

Until fairly recently few thinkers were feminists. The most obvious exception is the character Socrates in Plato's *Republic*.[25] In his dialogue, Socrates, discussing how to build a fine city-state, argues that both men and women should be educated and, if they prove to be competent, should become rulers of the state. This was a radical proposal, given the ancient Athenian view of women. But if we examine Socrates' argument closely, we detect some subtle but devastating challenges to the principle of political equality between men and women. Socrates proposes that, in order for the competent women to immerse themselves in politics completely and thus to keep up with their male fellow rulers ('guardians'), the private family would have to be abolished (*Republic* 457c–471b). The reason is simple: even though men and women might have roughly the same potential to participate in politics, they cannot be equally competent in actuality if women have to spend years feeding and raising children, which was a fact of life then as it still is, though maybe to a lesser extent, a fact of life today.[26] The underlying hypothesis is that spending time in the realm of private life is worthless for, if not detrimental to, public service. If this is the case, what appears to be an argument for political equality in leadership in the *Republic* poses at once a rather serious challenge to this equality: as long as the traditional family is intact, with women assuming the duties of pregnancy, giving birth and child-rearing (albeit with voluntary help from men), political equality in leadership is impossible.

However, as we have seen, early Confucians denied any simple divide between the private and the public. What is cultivated in private can be constructive for the public realm. Indeed, their defence of the principle of three years' mourning implicitly presupposes this understanding of private–public relations. That is, to spend three years remembering a parent (thereby reinvigorating one's filial love, and so forth) might help one become a better politician than might otherwise be the case. By the same rationale, a Confucian can argue that a female politician may well become a better leader through the experience of spending a few years raising her children. Thus, unlikely as it seems, from this perspective Confucian political philosophy can be interpreted as offering support for equality of the sexes in politics.[27]

The middle way of Confucianism: an equality-based mobile hierarchy

Having discussed early Confucian responses to the challenge of devising a new social glue for 'modern' states and dealing with the issue of international relations, and considered their implications both then and now, I move on in this chapter to discuss Confucians' engagement with the other crucial issue of modernity: finding a new mechanism to select members of the ruling class, including both the ruler and those in high office. Again, in addition to explicating their ideas, I will speculatively apply them to contemporary issues, especially those apparent in the liberal democracies. I will argue that some of their insights, reconstructed and applied to today's world, may well have the capacity to address contemporary issues more productively than the regime of liberal democracy.

Confucians' understanding of the equality of human beings

In their answer to the question of how to select the ruling class, we witness once again the Confucian 'middle way'. Nobility by birth was largely gone, but the inherited throne was still in place. Although many rulers were threatened by ambitious ministers, the institution of a powerful ruler presiding over a state was still strong – would-be usurpers did not challenge the institution itself, but only fought over who should be the head. How to determine the identity and scope of the ruling class was a pressing question. But, other than the inherited throne, interestingly, almost no prominent school from the pre-Qin era argued for a return to feudal hierarchy and nobility by birth. Pre-Qin Confucians were no exception. But they distinguished themselves from other schools by the form of equality that they advocated.

As indicated, Confucius is held to have been the first private teacher, publicly offering lessons in statecraft – hitherto the province of the nobility – to all. This was a daring move that further shook the foundations of feudal hierarchy. In the *Analects* (7.7), Confucius claims that, even if someone only had a meagre present for him, he has never denied him instruction. Elsewhere he makes his point more clearly: 'I educate everyone, and there are no distinctions', which presumably means no distinctions of class, wealth or origin (*Analects* 15.39).

Nevertheless, nowhere in the *Analects* does Confucius claim that everyone is equal in terms of their potential to be well educated, let alone become a sage-ruler. The idea that everyone should be educated might only suggest that everyone should have some education, or that we cannot predetermine who is and who is not educable. As we will see later in this chapter, this minimum presupposition may have been Confucius's position. Mencius and Xun Zi, however, went a step further by claiming that every human being is educable and has the potential to become a sage, in terms of morality if not wisdom. The famous passage about the falling child, quoted in the previous chapter, was part of Mencius's demonstration of the innate goodness of human nature. He claims that everything necessary for one's moral development is already in oneself (*Mencius* 7A4). That is, in terms of potential, human beings are all equal. In this sense, 'the sage and I are of the same kind' (6A7). The only difference between a sage and a common person is that the former is never oblivious to his original goodness, and cares to cultivate it to its fullest (4B12, 6A8, 6A11, 6A12, 6A18, 6A19 and 6A20).

A passage in the *Mencius* (6B2) nicely sums up Mencius's position on this matter. When asked if it is the case that all men are capable of becoming Yao and Shun, two sage-rulers that often serve as the ideal ruler and the ideal human being in the Confucian text, Mencius says yes. When pushed on the difference between these sage-rulers and a common man, Mencius answers that it is only a matter of effort. He continues:

> Here is a man whose strength cannot lift a chicken – he is then a man of no strength. Now if he lifted 100 jun [i.e. something really heavy], then he would be a man of strength. And so, whoever can lift the same weight as Wu Huo [a legendary heavy lifter] is himself a Wu Huo. Why should a man worry about a want of ability? It is only that he does not make an effort. To walk slowly, keeping behind his elders, is to show proper respect [ti 悌]. To walk quickly and overtake his elders is to fail to show proper respect. Now, is walking slowly what a man cannot do? It is what he does not do. The way of Yao and Shun is simply that of filial piety and the duty of being a respectful young man [ti]. If you wear the clothes of Yao, speak the words of Yao, and do the actions of Yao, and you will just be a Yao. And, if you wear the clothes of Jie [the last king of the Xia dynasty, allegedly a tyrant], speak the words of Jie, and do the actions of Jie, you will just be a Jie. (6B2)

Opposing Mencius's view of human nature, Xun Zi famously – or notoriously – denies the innate goodness of human beings, and argues that the goodness one has or the good deeds one does are the consequence of one's conscious efforts, cultivations and habituations (*Xun Zi*, Chapter 23). Xun Zi then argues that sage-rulers play a crucial role in establishing the rules and leading the masses down the right path. Nonetheless, in the same chapter, he affirms that anyone on the street can become a Yu, another legendary sage-ruler. He continues:

> I say that Yu was Yu [the sage-ruler] because he practised humanity, righteousness, laws and correct principles. It is the case that these can be known and practised [by all]. Everyone in the street

has the faculty to know them and has the capacity to practise them. Thus, it is clear that everyone in the street can be a Yu. ... Today, everyone in the street can know the right relations between father and son inside of his home [nei 内, literally 'inside'], and can know the correct relations between the ruler and the subjects outside of his home. Thus it is clear that everyone in the street has the faculty to know and the capacity to practise [the aforementioned four values practised by Yu]... (Xun Zi, Chapter 23; see Chan 1969: 133 for a partial English translation)

The argumentation that Xun Zi offers here is similar to that of Mencius in 6B2. But some subtle yet important differences remain. The ideal sage-rulers to whom Mencius likes to refer are Yao and Shun, while for Xun Zi it is Yu. As mentioned in Chapter 1, Yu gave his throne to one of his sons, while Yao and Shun did not. This might be why Yao and Shun, but not Yu, tend to serve as models for most Confucians. Another crucial difference is that Mencius emphasizes filial piety and brotherly respectfulness, and values innate and universal moral sentiment. In contrast, Xun Zi emphasizes laws and correct principles. He also likes to emphasize the role of li, not as internal moral regulation but as the external cultivation of correct conduct. These features are lacking in Mencius's discussions.

Interestingly, the *Analects* emphasize both the inner moral sentiment that lays the foundation of li and the external regulation that it offers. In this sense, Mencius and Xun Zi develop only one side of Confucius's views on li. On the hotly debated issue of whether human beings are innately good or bad, Confucius is curiously silent. The closest he comes to making a claim for human nature is the observation that 'by nature human beings are alike' (*Analects* 17.2), but he never asserts that we have a common nature and that this nature is good (or bad).[1] This may reflect the wisdom of Confucius: it is difficult to decide one way or the other on the issue of whether human beings are innately good or bad; in spite of the differences between Mencius and Xunzi, they agree on the need and the possibility for human beings to be good, which may be all that it is necessary to say on this issue. Thus we see that Confucius's position is midway between that of Mencius and of Xun Zi, at once synthesizing and transcending them.

Legitimacy of the sovereign
lies in satisfaction of the people's interests

In spite of their subtle differences, it is clear that early Confucians advocated some sort of equality. Their 'democratic' position did not stop here. They went on to address the issue of the sovereign's legitimacy, taking a similar attitude towards the common people, who in feudal times were looked down upon or disregarded. As we saw in Chapter 1, the legitimacy of the sovereign at this time was often founded on divine will, or the will or mandate of Heaven. With the collapse of feudalism, the issue of legitimacy re-emerged. Early Confucians' response was that it should lie in the satisfaction of people's interests.

A passage in the *Analects* (12.9) suggests that if people's basic needs are satisfied, so will the ruler's be. In the *Mencius*, there are many passages that made it abundantly clear that the satisfaction of people's basic interests confers ultimate legitimacy on the sovereign. In *Mencius* 5A5, in his discussion with a pupil of how Shun the sage-ruler was given the throne by his predecessor Yao, Mencius points out that 'the son of Heaven [the ruler] cannot give the world to another', but can only 'recommend a man to Heaven'. It is Heaven that gave the world to Shun. But 'Heaven does not speak but reveals itself through its acts and deeds', the ultimate source of which is the people; that is, 'Heaven sees with the eyes of its people; Heaven hears with the ears of its people.'

At another place, Mencius argues that when a ruler needs to decide which candidate is suitable or unsuitable for an office, and which official should be demoted or even punished with death, neither a consensus of those in his innermost circle nor that of the ministers is sufficient; only a consensus among the people would be jutification enough for the ruler to have the case investigated and for a decision to be reached. In the case of an official who stands to be punished by death, then, 'It is the people who put him to death. Only by acting in this manner can one be father and mother to the people' (*Mencius* 1B7). In short, for Mencius, the masses' interests always come first, before those of the rulers (7B14).

As we saw in Chapter 2, Mencius is explicit about the demand that the government be responsible for both the material and moral well-being of its people (*Mencius* 3A4). Moreover, for him, the moral well-being of the masses depends upon the satisfaction of their material interests:

> Only a member of the scholar-officials [shi 士][2] can have a constant [or 'stable'] heart in spite of a lack of constant means of support [or 'properties']. The people, on the other hand, will not have constant hearts if they are without constant means. Lacking constant hearts, they will go astray and fall into excess, stopping at nothing. To punish them after they have fallen foul of the law is to set a trap for the people. (*Mencius* 1A7; see also 3A3)

Implied here is that if people commit crimes on account of a lack of economic stability, the government should be held responsible, meaning that the government (as well as the criminal) should be punished for the crimes committed when the government fails to offer necessary goods to its people.[3]

Indeed, according to Mencius, if a ruler fails to deliver the service that he owes to the people, he should be removed, and even subjected to capital punishment. This was a message that no ruler liked to hear, but Mencius delivered it regardless. For example,

> Mencius said to King Xuan of Qi, 'Suppose one of Your Majesty's ministers were to entrust his wife and children to the care of a friend, while he himself went into Chu to travel, and that, upon his return, his friend had let his wife and children suffer from cold and hunger, then what should he do about it?'
> The King said, 'Break with his friend.'
> Mencius said, 'Suppose that the Marshal of the Guards was unable to keep his guards in order, then what should be done about it?'

The king said, 'Dismiss him.'

Mencius said, 'If the whole realm within the four borders [of your kingdom] is ill-governed, what should be done about it?'

The king looked to his right and left, and spoke of some other matters. (1B6)

Clearly, the message of this passage is that the ruler is responsible for good governance, and should be held accountable accordingly. And the ridiculing of King Quan of Qi is also plain to see.

Moreover, if a ruler who fails to do his duty should be removed, a tyrant, for his part, can even be punished with death. In a later passage, the same king asks,

'Is it true that Tang banished Jie [the last king of the Xia dynasty, who was said to be a tyrant] and King Wu marched against Zhou [the last king of the Shang dynasty, who was also said to be a tyrant]?'

'It is so recorded', answered Mencius.

'Is regicide permissible?'

'He who mutilates humanity is a mutilator; he who cripples righteousness is a crippler. A man who is both a mutilator and a crippler is a lone fellow [secluded from and abandoned by the people]. I have heard of killing the lone fellow Zhou, but have not heard of any regicide.' (1B8)

The hierarchical side of Confucianism

On the question of legitimacy, early Confucians might almost be taken for Enlightenment, even democratic, thinkers. But there are two subtle distinctions between the two positions. First, the basic interests of the people that need to be satisfied are not merely short-term material interests, but long-term material interests and moral needs. We learn in Mencius (3A4) that without the five basic human relations promoted by the government, we are not even human beings. So one might say that whereas for Confucians it is human interests that need to be satisfied, the contemporary focus on material interests serves only to satisfy the interests of the beasts.

Moreover, for Confucians, since human beings are intertwined with others through various social relations, especially family relations (filial piety towards parents and ancestors, concern for children and future generations), humans have connections with people who have passed away and people who haven't been born. Thus for Confucians 'human interests' have a historical dimension, and are not exclusively the realm of living human beings. Second, we learn (particularly in 3A4) that Confucians consider government a source of good, and not a necessary (or even unnecessary) evil, as many modern Western thinkers, such as Thomas Hobbes in *Leviathan* and Rousseau in his praise of the noble savage in *Discourse on the Origin and Foundations of Inequality* (*The Second Discourse*), have believed.

More importantly, early Confucians also have a non-egalitarian and non-democratic side, which may even appear to be in conflict with the profile described thus far. In spite of his insistence on our moral capacity to become a sage, Mencius equally forcefully insists upon the distinction between great men and 'small men' (*xiaoren* 小人). Let us consider what he says in the very long 3A4 section of the *Mencius*, a passage to which we have already referred. The section starts by describing another school of people, the leader of which was Xu Xing 许行, who by all accounts preached the teachings of Shen Nong 神农, a legendary figure who is credited with the invention of agriculture.[4] The ideas of this school seem to be radically egalitarian. People of this school strove by themselves to satisfy their basic needs, rather than taking advantage of the service of others. They all dressed, lived and ate in a rather simple manner. They heard that the Duke Wen of Teng, whom we came across earlier, was a humane ruler, and decided to become his subjects. Chen Xiang, a pupil of Chen Liang, a Confucian, and his younger brother also heard about Duke Wen and likewise became his subjects. When Chen Xiang met with Xu Xing, he was so pleased with his teachings that he abjured his previous – Confucian – lessons and became a follower of Xu Xing. Chen Xiang later visited Mencius, and reported to him what Xu Xing had said about Duke Wen of Teng:

The Duke of Teng is indeed a good and wise ruler. Nevertheless, he hasn't been taught the Way. A [truly] wise ruler tills the land together with his people and then eats [his share], and governs while cooking his own meals. Now Teng has granaries and treasuries. This is to inflict hardship on the people in order to provide for [the ruler] himself. How can he be a good and wise ruler? (3A4)

In addressing the political issues of the day, the Xu Xing school believed that everyone should lead a simple life and be self-sufficient. By so doing, we can do away with exploitation and war, thereby achieving world peace.

Mencius rejects this philosophy. First, he shows that Xu Xing would not be able to make everything on his own. For example, he could not have woven the cap he wore because to do so would have interfered with his farming. Also, he had to trade grain for cooking utensils and farming tools. Furthermore, to trade for all these things would clearly not inflict hardship on those who produce them. Likewise, the artisans who trade what they produce for grain would not be inflicting hardship on the farmers. The reason is offered by Chen Liang, who is pushed by Mencius to realize that 'Of course, one cannot till the land and do the work of a hundred different crafts together.' Mencius concludes:

Now, is ruling the world such an exception that it can be done together with farming? There are affairs of great men, and there are affairs of small men.... There are those who use their minds and there are those who use their muscles. The former rule; the latter are ruled. Those who rule are supported by those who are ruled. This is a principle accepted by the world. (3A4)

In this passage, the term 'great men' (daren 大人) could refer to members of the ruling class. If we recall the passage quoted in the previous chapter (Analects 9.11), in which someone asks why if Confucius was a sage he could do so many lowly things, we observe that it was customary to think that someone of the ruling class was not supposed to do menial tasks.

However, as I have argued, Confucian conservatism with regard to received customs may have been more apparent than real. Here in 3A4, we see that Mencius tries to offer an explanation or interpretation of the idea that great men shouldn't be involved in menial tasks. The obvious reason he gives is the necessity of the division of labour. For one human being simply cannot produce everything that he or she needs in his or her life, however simple that life is. But Mencius also seems to think that the work of the ruling class and that of the ruled are not merely the product of the division of labour. For he calls members of the ruling class 'great men', and the ruled 'small men'. He offers no explicit reason. Yet if we recall Mencius's general teachings, we know that what defines a human is his compassion (*Mencius* 2A6). It follows that the job of ruling (i.e. helping all human beings in one's own country, and by extension in the whole world) is the deepest expression of this defining human characteristic. In contrast, labouring utilizing one's muscles, if it serves one's own interest, is essentially no different from the activities of animals; and if it serves the interests of others it is still inferior to ruling, as menial work cannot benefit as many people as ruling. In later passages of 3A4, Mencius makes it clear that the job of 'great men' is to focus on promoting the material and moral well-being of 'small men', the masses. It is true that Mencius's defence of hierarchy may well offend contemporary sensibilities, but it is clear that for Mencius the justification for someone to be a member of the elite is his capacity and willingness to serve the non-elite.

Towards the end of this long section, Chen Liang attempts one last defence of Xu Xing's teachings: if the price of a quantity of goods is the same, he says, deception will disappear. Mencius answers:

> that things are unequal [in terms of their quality] is a matter of fact.... If you rank them the same, it will bring confusion to the world. If a roughly finished shoe sells at the same price as a finely finished one, who would make the latter? Following the way of Master Xu is to lead each other to deception. How can one govern a state in this way?

Thus, notwithstanding Mencius's belief that every human has the capacity to become a sage, he seems also to believe that, in practice, only a few people can realize their potential. This inequality in practice is for Mencius a fact of life. If we attempt to suppress this fact of inequality in the world, it will return in an even worse form. The Confucian wisdom, then, is that, given inequality is inevitable, instead of hopelessly and counterproductively trying to eliminate it, we should turn it into something good – in the service of 'small men', the disadvantaged.[5] To adapt the American political philosopher John Rawls's idea of a 'difference principle', according to which economic inequality is tolerated if it serves the most disadvantaged the best (Rawls 1971: 75–83), we can understand the Confucian idea as a 'political difference principle'.

Some Chinese commentators in the current and the last century have argued that Confucianism and socialism are compatible.[6] The two schools certainly share a compassion for the poor. However, Confucians maintain that care for the poor cannot be promoted by an equality imposed from above. One clear example is China before and during the Cultural Revolution, when radical equality imposed by the Communist Party led to a society in which although most people were indeed equal, so were they equally poor, and in which one man (Chairman Mao) or a group of men (the Party elite) enjoyed great privileges over the many. Other examples are the economic inequality in South Korea and Japan, on the one hand, and in the USA, on the other. South Korea and Japan retain elements of the Confucian heritage in their culture of respecting seniority (in terms of position in a company or the government), whereas in the USA the sense of equality is deeply rooted in the American psyche. However, economic inequality in the USA is much greater than it is in Japan and South Korea.[7] As with any political issue, the causes of this difference are myriad and complicated, but one possible cause might be as follows. If Confucians are correct in their understanding that we human beings are hierarchical by nature – that is, we wish to excel relative to others – then this will be expressed in one form or another. In Japan and South Korea, CEOs can satisfy their hierarchical desires with people's respect. In the USA, however, since everyone is considered equal, CEOs have to prove their superiority by other means. Since all other avenues for the expression of hierarchy are largely closed off on account of the formal equality of all, the most convenient way left is to show off through the base and naked display of means – that is, money and material possessions. This is perhaps one reason why CEOs in the USA have a greater appetite for wealth than those in Japan and South Korea. If this is the case, the question we should ask ourselves is: if inequality is inevitable, which form of it do we prefer? I consider the Confucian answer that doesn't attempt to eliminate inequality in vain, but instead focuses on discovering and constructing an inequality that benefits the least advantaged the most, a wise one.

Although he was the first private teacher who did not discriminate against those with no wealth or social status, Confucius seemed to believe in some form of hierarchy and made statements that might offend today's democratic ear. He was insistent that not everyone is educable. For him, 'human beings are similar in nature, but apart by habit'; moreover, 'only the most wise and the most stupid cannot be moved' (Analects 17.2, 17.3). Furthermore, in his view it is not only the most stupid who are ineducable. He warned that 'you can acquaint those above the average with higher things, but you cannot acquaint those below the average with them' (Analects 6.21). Hence, the masses 'can be made to follow, but not to know' (Analects 8.9).

Now, how can we reconcile the practice of the first private teacher with his call to limit the scope of education? A similar conundrum, touched on above but not satisfactorily resolved, is Mencius's insistence both on human equality in terms of potential and on the necessity of hierarchy. One possible answer is that government fails to provide the necessary conditions for all to develop their potential. But to sanction inequality on account of government failure would be considered by many to be unjust, Confucians among them.

As we have seen, early Confucians believed that the government should be responsible for the material and spiritual well-being of its people. This means that the government should provide food, shelter and education to all. In the case of political participation, Mencius considers this a specialist job, and thus leisure should also be provided to participants by the government. Mencius's insistence on the justifiability of hierarchy, then, implies the following. If some people fail to realize their potential due to the government's failure, this can be considered an injustice, and should be corrected. However, the reality is that, regardless of the government's efforts, not everyone can achieve the status of 'great man', on account of contingent factors beyond human control – the nature of which Mencius does not make explicit. For want of a better explanation, we must consider this to have been a fact of life for Mencius and a basic premiss in his philosophy.

The case of Confucius is different. For he never claimed that we human beings are equal in terms of our potential or capacities. Although Mencius may well have believed the same, Confucius explicitly states that those who actually turn out to be wise and virtuous are few in number. Moreover, Mencius tends to be optimistic regarding the possibility of 'great men' emerging from the masses, whereas Confucius, for his part, was not too sanguine about human beings. In the *Analects* (4.6), Confucius observes that he has never met a man who likes humanity or despises inhumanity. He has never seen a man who applied his strength to the practice of humanity for a single day, and this was not through lack of strength. In *Analects* 7.26, Confucius says that he never hopes to see a good man, but only a man who has 'constancy' (*heng* 恒). In two passages, Confucius tells us: 'I haven't met a man who likes virtue as much as physical beauty' (9.18, 15.13). Although it seems to be a basic requirement for rulers to be generous towards people and able to help the masses, Confucius considered these qualities to be so difficult to obtain that even Yao and Shun, personifying the highest ideals in Confucian rulers, could not fulfil expectations (6.29, 6.30).

Thus Confucius thought that to be truly humane is a lofty goal, and a state that only a few, if any, are able to achieve. One reason seems to be the weakness of the human will, which seems unable to resist temptation (as in Confucius's example concerning 'physical beauty') and cannot muster the strength to be virtuous. It is also likely that Confucius did not accept to begin with that human beings possess equal capacities. Meanwhile, Confucius likely thought that, first, everyone needs some kind of education, and, second, we cannot predetermine who is capable of receiving the highest level of education. This might explain why, in spite of Confucius's lack of confidence in the human capacity to be good, he strongly advocates some form of 'mass education'.

Although Confucius and Mencius had different reasons to believe that people are unequal in actuality, they both accepted it as a fact of life. Both considered it dangerous for people of lesser ability to usurp the duties of those with greater aptitude. Their insistence on the importance of hierarchy then serves the political purpose of maintaining order. At the same time, we note that neither Confucius nor Mencius saw this order as predetermined, and thus they supported upward mobility and social fluidity. The apparent conflict between what can be considered the egalitarian and the elitist values in Confucius and Mencius, then, reflects their attempts to address two fundamental needs in politics: order (stability) and upward mobility (fluidity).

A similar concern can be found in Plato's *Republic*. Socrates daringly proposes educating not just every man, but also every woman, whom most Ancient Greeks considered to be inherently unstable and therefore disqualified from education. Then, curiously, after tests are given to the students (being the means by which the ruling class is chosen) Socrates proposes that a noble lie be told to all, part of which is to convince people of the following: that rulers are chosen not on the basis of their educational performance and test results – in fact they received no education; rather, they are chosen based upon the metal they were born with (*Republic* 414b–415d). Socrates explicitly states that this is a lie because education is given to every young person. Yet Socrates may have also thought that this mass education should not be open-ended, and should be curtailed for the sake of order and stability; this could have been one motivation for the noble lie.

But a crucial difference exists between the Confucian effort to find a middle way between fluidity and stability and that in the *Republic*. In the *Republic*, fluidity, especially upward mobility, is brought to an absolute stop when the noble lie is told. From then on, the masses can never move up the social ladder. For Confucians, although there is a hierarchy that should be respected and maintained, the door to the ruling class is never shut to the masses. This is partly due to the continuous interactions that Confucians perceive in the relations between the private and the public, which we discussed in the previous chapter. Moreover, early Confucians' perception of moral cultivation is also one of fluidity and continuity. In another early Confucian classic, *Zhong Yong* 中庸 (traditionally translated as *The Doctrine of the Mean*), this characterization is offered:

> The way of the exemplary person [*junzi*] is everywhere yet hidden. Man and wife of simple intelligence can know it, and yet in its utmost reaches there is something which even the sage does not know. Man and wife of no moral character can put it into practice, and yet in its utmost reaches there is something which even the sage is not able to put into practice. ... The way of the exemplary person has its simple beginnings in [the relations between] man and wife, but in its utmost reaches it is clearly seen in Heaven and Earth. (*Zhong Yong* Chapter 12, my translation; cf. Chan 1969: 100)

The Confucian hybrid regime

The question therefore arises: how is the hierarchical picture in *Mencius* 3A4 to be reconciled with the more 'populist' message in *Mencius* 1B6, 1B7, 1B8, 5A5 and 7B14, in which Mencius appears to argue that the legitimacy of the sovereign's rule stems from the popular will? We should first be clear about certain subtle points

in Mencius's message. In 7B14, Mencius confirms that people are
the prime concern, but he does not say that political matters should
therefore be decided by the people. In 1B6 and 1B8, he suggests that
a ruler who fails to serve the people should be removed or even put
to death, but he does not indicate that people should do the removing
or the killing. In 1B7, he advises that, regarding the promotion or
demotion of a minister, a consensus among either his innermost
circle or ministers is not enough; only a wider consensus among the
people would justify the ruler investigating the case and reaching a
decision. But notably he does not say that such a popular consensus
should lead directly to promotion or demotion. Rather, the ruler has
to play an executive role. In 5A5, Mencius denies that it was Yao who
gave the throne to Shun; rather, it was the doing of Heaven, and
Heaven hears and sees through people. So Shun was not popularly
elected by the people; Yao recommended him to Heaven and let Shun
demonstrate his ability to the people. Thereafter Shun assisted Yau for
twenty-eight years, which afforded the people plenty of opportunity
to learn who he was. Then and only then, after Yao had died, did
the people choose to follow Shun instead of Yao's son.

Thus, from a closer look at these passages, Mencius's subtle messages become clear. The legitimacy of the sovereign does depend on
people's satisfaction. But people may not be the best judges of how
and why they are satisfied or dissatisfied. The reason is offered in
Mencius 3A4, where Mencius implicitly explains the rationale of rule
over 'small men'. As we have seen, he argues that great men cannot
be involved in daily chores because their time is consumed by their
political duties. The flip side of this argument, then, is that small
men, who do not enjoy freedom from daily chores, cannot think
productively about political matters. Mencius is referring mainly to
those doing menial jobs. But by this criterion, many contemporary
'white-collar' professionals, such as scientists, engineers, doctors,
financiers, teachers, and so on – those whom José Ortega y Gasset
called 'learned ignorami' – should also be included in the category
of 'small men', because many are consumed by their daily work,

and are likely to possess limited knowledge of public affairs or of matters outside their narrow specializations (Ortega y Gasset 1932: 108–12). Thus, according to Mencius, it is almost impossible for the working class to make sound political decisions, as their judgements are either based upon narrow and immediate self-interest and partisanship, or are misdirected by demagogues. As the *Mencius* (5A5) makes clear, even during the Yao–Shun time, when the state was fairly small, it still took twenty-eight years for people to understand who Shun was. In terms of the judgement of who or what policies will promote or harm people's interests, therefore, the opinions of the 'great men' – those who are wise and compassionate – should play a large role.

Therefore, according to Mencius, although satisfaction of the people's basic needs is the ultimate ground of legitimacy of a state, the involvement of a ruling elite is necessary. But that ruling elite is not the same as the status quo, the powers that be. Rather, its members should be the wise and compassionate, the 'nobility by merit', and it is they who should replace the rule of nobility by birth that constituted the ruling class before the SAWS. The true ruling elite, the meritocrats, are few in number. According to Mencius, the masses are many, but they fail to develop their wisdom and virtue fully, thus lacking either the necessary political wisdom or the willingness to participate in politics in a constructive manner. They are also consumed by their daily chores. Their active involvement in politics should thus be balanced by the political involvement of the ruling elite, who are selected from the people by proving themselves to be wise and virtuous. Hence, the ideal government for Mencius is a hybrid of two components: the popular (democratic) and the elite (meritocratic).

Mencius says little about how to institutionalize the ideal government. Indeed, a concern with institutions was not his strong suit. It is the Legalists who paid more attention to such issues. But let us do a thought experiment, and imagine what kind of institutions Mencius would propose were he alive.[8] There are many possibilities.

One is a bicameral congress structure that consists of a popularly elected chamber and a chamber whose members are selected through examination or recommendation. The members of the latter chamber might include, for example, the heads of reputable NGOs and retired state officials with a good track record in office. Chinese history, another source of inspiration on this matter, shows that many ways of selecting the meritocrats were tried and practised. I discuss some of these in Chapter 6, along with other related arrangements that promote checks and balances, fairness, and so on.[9]

The terms 'elite' and 'meritocracy' might jar on today's democratic ears because, in the West, they imply inherited status, and suggest a sense of disenfranchisement and resentment. But since the SAWS, partly thanks to its promotion by Confucians, upward mobility has been cut deep into the Chinese psyche. This is reflected in the famous line of an ancient Chinese poem: 'one can be a farm boy in the morning, but come to the emperor's court in the evening' (朝为田舍郎, 暮登天子堂). Although few people actually become rulers, the door is nevertheless open to everyone and the government has a duty to support this principle. Moreover, the justification for one's politically superior status comes from the commitment to serving those of an inferior standing. This may help dispel the resentment often associated with meritocracy.

The Confucian hybrid regime may have implications for today's political world. In my view, today's democracies face four problems.[10] First, the official ideology of many democracies tends to be a radical version of individualism. This ideology places too much confidence in the citizenry and encourages mistrust of government and the ruling elite. Second, democracies, in their reliance on the institution of one person, one vote, tend to neglect the interests of non-voters, such as past and future generations (which is one reason why budget deficits and the issue of the environment are so difficult to solve) and foreigners (which impacts on foreign aid and diplomacy). Third, even in terms of present voters' interests, the powerful and vocal tend to suppress the powerless and silent, especially when liberties are not well protected by the rule of law. This is a root cause of ethnic violence and can lead to government policies being hijacked by the extreme wings of political parties. Fourth, even in terms of (vocal) voters' own interests, the masses' lack of political understanding and judgement in today's democracies is an established fact in political science.[11] These factors render the popular vote alone a far from ideal method of selecting legislators.

Some democratic thinkers acknowledge these problems, and consequently attempt to correct the system from within, such as improving economic equality and educational provision (including civics, to cultivate mutual respect among and beyond the citizenry), keeping voters informed, eradicating the influence of money in politics, and so on.[12] Confucians would heartily endorse these methods, because they are also exactly what Confucian political philosophy teaches. But they also maintain that this internal tinkering is not enough; Confucian and meritocratic elements must be added if such problems are to be resolved. For, in my view, the shortcomings of the popular vote are deeply rooted in the modern world and cannot be put to rights within the present democratic system. The reasons, very simply put, are as follows. Almost every contemporary state manifests two fundamental conditions. First, most states are very large in comparison to the scale of Ancient Athens, the first democratic state in human history. Again, in politics, size matters. When a state is small, its affairs are easy to grasp, and the room for political manipulation is slight. Furthermore, the opportunity to amass a large sum of wealth is unlikely to be present. In contrast, the affairs of a large state are hard to grasp, even for the experts. The big corporations enabled by the advent of the large state and the globalized world have developed interests different from those of the people within a state, any state. They have the motivation and the power to distort political information to serve their interests. Second, almost all contemporary states are capitalistic in terms of their economic system, meaning that almost everyone is consumed by their specialized job. Pluralism and tolerance in contemporary liberal states also do not encourage people to devote their limited free time to politics, but allow them to pursue their own interests. In contrast, Ancient Athenians enjoyed the leisure that was bestowed on them by slavery – slaves performed their daily chores – and they were forced to be involved in politics, such as participating in events such as wars.

Most contemporary liberal thinkers agree that, for people to participate meaningfully in politics, they have to meet some basic criteria, such as being informed and demonstrating basic moral values such as reciprocity and fairness.[13] However, what we have designated the two constitutive conditions of the modern state preclude the possibility of the masses meeting the criteria that even liberal thinkers consider essential for democracy to function. In this regard, Confucians would argue that they are justified in insisting upon adding meritocratic elements to the political regime.

By adding meritocratic elements to the political regime, we can balance the voice of uninformed and politically unsophisticated voters in both domestic and international affairs. For the Confucian elite – those who hold to the basic ideas of Confucianism, rather than those trained in the Confucian classics – may be able to endorse policies that are in the voters' interests, broadly construed (including their short- and long-term material interests, as well as moral needs that are thin enough to be in the public sphere and are essential for a healthy democracy), and policies for the greater good (taking in the interests of past and future generations and of foreigners). This is on account of the Confucian understanding of humanity (with compassion at its core), of universal but hierarchical love, of the social nature of human beings (hence the ability to weigh the impact of long-term policies), and so on. A strengthened voice of the Confucian in the legislature and in political matters in general may thus, according to Confucian thinking, promote good policymaking in key areas.

However, Confucians would not argue for the removal of the popular voice in politics. What they advocate is a hybrid regime, preserving the good elements of popular democracy (such as the rule of law; protection of basic liberties; checks and balances, especially those mediating relations between the elite and the masses), while attempting to balance its overemphasis on the popular will with a meritocratic component. The Confucian meritocracy is also rooted in the principle of upward mobility, which may serve further to dispel feelings of resentment from the masses; for it requires that the government provide basic goods to the masses, including the necessary conditions for them to participate in politics; furthermore, anyone, if he or she is so willing, can become a member of the ruling class through tests. More generally, if modern democracy emerged as a way to counter the abuse of the nobles, perhaps the time has come to counter the abuse of the uninformed and not-so-virtuous masses with meritocrats.

Some may argue that there are already meritocratic elements in today's democracies.[14] This may well be true. But, first, some of these elements are not meritocratic in a Confucian way. For example, the wealthy are often disproportionately represented among politicians, which actually makes them plutocrats; whereas for Confucians the relevant merits are political wisdom and compassion for others. Second, the leaders in today's democracies – be they members of Congress in the USA, parliamentarians in the UK, or politicians in France – are often far better educated than the masses, which (partially) meets the Confucian criteria of meritocracy. However, on account of the dominant democratic mores, especially in the United States, the mechanism for selecting leaders comes rather close to populism; government is considered a necessary or even an unnecessary evil, and any sign of superiority will be abhorred by the masses. As a consequence, American politicians in particular often seek people's vote with a pledge to destroy the evil government, for all those in office are portrayed as a bunch of crooks. It is small wonder, then, that the most democratically elected congress is the institution respected least by the people, less than the not-directly-elected military, the appointed Supreme Court and the Federal Reserve (Zakaria 2003:

248; Bell 2006: 289 n34). Democratic politicians also contrive to hide their superior education from the people, working hard to win the contest among politicians of posing as an ordinary Joe. Such manoeuvres are poisonous to good governance. Democratic mores aside, the fact that these politicians are voted for by uninformed and self-interested voters constrains those who wish to do the right, but not necessarily the popular, thing.

The Confucian meritocracy, by contrast, takes the government as a necessary good. When politicians do their job properly, they should be respected. Elections, for Confucians, are not to get rid of the bad, but to select the good, which can help inform the tone of elections. Thus this model of meritocracy offers healthier mores than the putative democratic one. More importantly, since the meritocrats in this regime are not popularly elected but are selected through other means (examinations, etc.), they may be in a better position to carry through policies that are necessary but not popular. At the same time, the democratic elements (for example, the popularly elected chamber of a bicameral legislature) can serve as a check and balance to this meritocratic branch. Hence the Confucian hybrid regime tries to find a middle way between the popular and the competent, and may offer a better model of good government than today's democracies.

FOUR

Daoism:
return to an age of innocence

Having considered the responses of Confucians to the issues arising from the advent of modernity in China, we will now discuss
the approach taken by another school of political thought. As we
have seen, early Confucians have sometimes been portrayed as
reactionaries, but this does not do them justice. For, in spite of
their apparent conservatism, they faced the problems of modernity
head-on, embracing the new by reinterpreting the old. There are,
however, good grounds for arguing that the early Daoists, especially
their purported founding master, Lao Zi, were the true reactionaries.
They argue that a return to the premodern stage is the only viable
solution to the problems of modernity. In support of this contention,
they also subject Confucian designs to critique. Their ideas have
found resonance with certain modern European thinkers as well as
with contemporary movements; thus to understand Daoism is also,
to a degree, to gain some insight into both the nature and merits
of a particular strand of European thought and what motivates those
in the aforementioned contemporary movements.

Difficulties in understanding the *Lao Zi*

First, let me say a few words about the presumed founder of this school, Lao Zi. As we have seen, Zi means master. *Lao* was an unusual family name; literally it means 'old'. Hence 'Lao Zi' can simply mean 'Old Master'. This seems a fitting name for 'him', for 'his' teachings were indeed a call to return to the good old days. Quotation marks are placed around 'he' and 'his' here because we cannot be sure who Lao Zi was, or indeed whether there was ever such a person. The historical record is sketchy and often internally contradictory. In one record (*Shiji* Volume 47) it is said that Confucius once asked about li (rites and rituals) to a court historian named Lao Zi. But this record is of doubtful reliability, and indeed whether this Lao Zi is the Daoist under discussion here remains an open question. One of the more outlandish accounts of Lao Zi is the following (Fung 1966: 241). The biography of Lao Zi in *Shiji* relates that he disappeared and no one knew his whereabouts. When Buddhism was introduced to China, many intellectuals could not accept the fact that there existed a civilization as sophisticated as the Chinese. These intellectuals apparently saw similarities between the Buddhist sutras and the *Lao Zi*. So the story was invented that Lao Zi had visited the West, and while there had taught the Buddha and his pupils. For how else could it be explained that unheard-of individuals, who, since they were not Chinese, could not possibly be civilized, could come up with a system of teachings like Buddhism?

Hence, whether or not Lao Zi the person ever existed is a somewhat controversial issue. Those who admire Daoism tend, of course, to believe that he indeed lived; furthermore they like to believe that he pre-dated Confucius, which would boost the status of Daoism. I won't enter into this controversy, but will simply assume that Lao Zi the person may not have lived. For, in truth, all we have is the book titled *Lao Zi*, or *Dao De Jing*. There is also controversy over which version is the original and authentic text. Naturally, when the text differs from one version to another, the meaning may also differ. Again, I will leave this question aside. The version I use is the commonly received one, edited and with commentary by Wang Bi 王弼 (226–249).[1]

Notwithstanding this avoidance of certain controversy, difficulties remain. The *Lao Zi* is a short book (about 5,000 Chinese characters) composed of aphorisms and mystical or apparently counter-intuitive expressions. For example, the book opens with the line 'The Dao [Way] that can be told of is not the eternal Dao',[2] and then proceeds to tell the reader what Dao is. This has prompted confusion, and even opened the book up to ridicule. The famed Tang intellectual and poet Bai Juyi 白居易 even wrote a poem, 'Reading the *Lao Zi*', to articulate this sense. It reads:

> Those who speak do not know, and those who know do not speak,
>   this I heard from Lao Zi.
> But if Lao Zi is said to be someone who knows,
> Why did he himself write a book of five thousand characters?[3]

One way to solve the riddle is to claim that there are different ways of speaking. The opening line of the *Lao Zi* only rejects the notion that the message of the book can be communicated in one manner, perhaps the ordinary manner of speaking. But there are other ways to express the ineffable without falling into the trap of ordinary modes of speaking or address. Be that as it may, in order to make the text sensible to the reader, I will have to discuss the *Lao Zi* in an analytical and 'ordinary' manner. All I can strive to do is make sure my interpretation is consistent, while not implying that it is necessarily the correct interpretation of the *Lao Zi*.

Moreover, because the *Lao Zi* is a short and aphoristic text, and because (unlike the case of the *Analects*, which is also short and aphoristic) we know little of its author(s) and have few comparable contemporaneous texts, and thus little information to help us shed light on the meanings of passages, the issue of punctuation is more critical than is the case with other classical Chinese texts. Here, again, I rely on the authoritative Wang Bi version of the *Lao Zi*.

Why can't taking action cure political ills?

As discussed in the previous two chapters, faced with the chaos occasioned by China's transition to modernity, early Confucians introduced the notion of humanity. The caring feeling towards strangers was to act as the new social glue. If this moral sentiment were to develop fully, the world would be a better place. Moreover, to achieve peace and prosperity, we need wise and virtuous people to take action, even if a task is deemed impossible and hopeless. For example, after a pupil of Confucius told a gatekeeper that he came from Confucius's home, the gatekeeper said this of Confucius: 'Is he the one who knows that something cannot be done, but does it anyway?' (14.38). In spite of the tone of gentle ridicule, this portrait may well have been accurate of Confucius and, indeed, Confucians. Zeng Zi, a good pupil of Confucius, said,

> A scholar-official must be strong and resolute, for his burden is heavy and the road is long. He takes humanity as his own burden. Isn't it heavy? Only with death does he stop [on the road to save the world]. Isn't that long? (*Analects* 8.7)

Yet for the early Daoists, human emotions and ambitions were not the solution but the root cause of the problems of the day. According to Mencius, Yang Zhu 杨朱, an influential thinker during the SAWS era whom some considered a Daoist, possibly even the earliest known Daoist (Fung 1966: 60–67), is supposed to have claimed that 'even if he could benefit the world by pulling out one hair [of his], he would not do it' (*Mencius* 7A26). Mencius explains that Yang Zhu made this claim on account of his egoism. Yet it seems strange that such egoistic teaching could be so influential at that time. In another text – commonly considered to be not authentic but, rather, forged by later writers – in which a chapter allegedly recorded sayings by Yang Zhu, a passage reads:

> If by damaging a single hair they could have benefited the world, the men of antiquity would not have done it. Had the world been

offered to them as their possession, they would not have taken
it. If everybody would refuse to pull out one hair, and everybody
would refuse to benefit the world, then the world would be in
order. (Yang Zhu chapter of the *Lie Zi*; for another English translation, see Chan 1969: 311)

The last line of this passage reveals something more than a merely
egoistic or selfish doctrine. The call to refrain from acting for the
benefit of the world, according to this passage, may actually benefit it.
The reason that the world is in chaos is that there are too many fakes
and phonies who pretend to help others, but actually take advantage
of them. Even if those who claim they are trying to save the world
are sincere, like the Confucians, they are actually perpetuating chaos
by their insistence on competition (between what they consider good
and what they consider bad).

For example, many believe that the reason the USA invaded Iraq
was for control of the oil in the Middle East, notwithstanding the
claim by some Americans that the motivation was the liberation of
the Iraqi people. Similar pretences were often used during the SAWS
era when one state attacked another. Confucian justifications for
war could well offer ambitious rulers the opportunity for pretence.
Moreover, to take the example of the Iraq War, even if pro-war
American politicians sincerely believed in the war of liberation, from
the above passage's point of view they might have made the situation
worse regardless of their good intentions. For the war of liberation
is based upon a sense of good and evil, and this will serve to stir
up others – for example, the Iraqis wronged during the Iraq War
or al-Qaeda members – to fight for what they consider just, be it
revenge on Americans for the deaths of the Iraqis in the war or the
liberation of Arabs from the evils of American ideology.

Whether the passage quoted above does indeed represent the belief
of Yang Zhu and was close to what he actually said is impossible to
say. But it does echo ideas in the *Lao Zi*. According to this text, good
and bad, or other opposing pairs, have value relative to each other.
Chapter 2 of the *Lao Zi* reads:

When the world knows beauty as beauty, there [arises the recognition of] ugliness. When they all know the good as good, there [arises the recognition of] evil.

[Thus,] being [*you* 有] and non-being [*wu* 无][4] produce each other...

Therefore, the sage manages affairs with non-action [*wu wei* 无 为] and practises the teachings of no words. All things arise [on their own], and he does not initiate [this process]; he produces and nurtures them, but does not take possession of them; he acts, but does not rely [on his own ability]; he accomplishes his task, but does not claim credit for it. It is precisely because he does not claim credit that his accomplishment stays with him.

Indeed, to call someone beautiful presupposes that someone else, imagined or real, can be considered ugly. Thus the existence of, for example, beauty, produces its opposite, ugliness. Generally, opposites produce each other. When we pursue something beautiful, it will stop satisfying us and turn ugly when we discover that there is something even more beautiful out there. Failing to see the relative nature of a pair of opposites and having access to new things will lead to perpetual competition and wars.

Moreover, according to the *Lao Zi*, the good and the bad always accompany each other, and the wheel of fortune contunues to turn, in spite of human desires. A passage in Chapter 58 reads: 'Disaster is that upon which good fortune rests, and good fortune is that beneath which disaster is hidden.' A famous story in a later text illustrates this point beautifully (*Huai Nan Zi* Volume 18; Liu 1986: 311). A horse that belonged to a good rider living near the border ran away to a barbarous area. When others expressed sympathy, the father of this rider commented, 'How could this not be good fortune?' A few months later, the runaway horse returned, bringing with it several good horses. On being congratulated, the father said, 'How could this not be a disaster?' His son liked to ride these new horses, but one day broke a leg when doing so. When others again expressed sympathy, the father said, 'How could this not be good fortune?' A year later, the barbarians attacked; many young men were drafted to fight. Most of them died. But because the son of the old man was crippled, he was not required to go to war and thus was spared.

Therefore we cannot have one thing without having the opposite, because each of a pair of opposites accompanies the other. We cannot hold on to only one of the pair, because it is in the process of constantly changing into its opposite. Indeed, 'returning is how the Way moves' (Lao Zi Chapter 40). The cyclic movement is the Dao or the way of things that cannot be violated. We can illustrate this with another passage from the Lao Zi:

> To be sparing with words is natural.
> So, a whirlwind does not last a whole morning, and a heavy
>   downpour does not last all day.
> What produces these? Heaven and Earth.
> Even Heaven and Earth cannot keep things going for a long time,
>   let alone humans!
> This is why one should follow the Way in all that one does.
>   (Chapter 23)

According to the Lao Zi, nature moves in the way it moves; human beings are incapable of making any real changes to its course. If we try to do so, it will have an adverse effect. Metaphorically speaking, nature is like a slow-flowing river. It flows slightly faster here, and more slowly there. But overall it is a gently flowing river. But people do not like it. Out of a mistaken sense of power, they wish to stop the river flowing. So they build a dam. But, unfortunately, due to their incompetence, the dam they build is too weak to hold for long. So, one day, when the dam collapses, in place of the gently flowing river they did not like they will face the horrors of a flood. Therefore,

> When alive the human [body] is tender and weak, and when dead
>   it is stiff and strong....
> Therefore the stiff and the strong belong to death, while the tender
>   and the weak belong to life.
> This is why a weapon that is strong will not win, and a tree that is
>   too strong will break.

The strong and the great reside down below, while the tender and the weak reside on top. (Chapter 76)

According to the *Lao Zi*, most human beings do not understand the relative and symbiotic nature of a pair of opposites, and do not know that they cannot change their eternally turning nature. With the acquisition of increasing amounts of positive knowledge and thus assuming a false sense of human capacities and power, they fool-hardily strive to change the course of nature. In this regard, human knowledge is but profound ignorance in disguise, and is a danger to human beings. True knowledge, in contrast, lies in the recognition of our fundamental ignorance and inadequacy – fundamental because we cannot change this aspect of human life. This position contrasts with Socrates' conception of human ignorance: in the Platonic dialogues he never stops trying to gain (positive) knowledge, which is predicated on the assumption that human beings can hope to obtain true (positive) knowledge. This is perhaps why the *Lao Zi* celebrates ignorance (which is true knowledge) and denounces positive and constructive human knowledge (which is really ignorance). Chapter 20 reads:

Cut off learning and there will be no worry!
... How much difference is there between the beautiful and the
    ugly? ...
The multitude are merry ... I alone am still and inactive, showing
    no sign [of joy], like a child who has not yet learned to smile...
I have the mind of a fool, listless and indiscriminate!
The common folk are bright, and I alone am dull.
The common folk are clever and discriminating, and I alone make
    no distinctions. ...
The multitude all have something to do, and I alone remain
    obstinate and immobile...

Here we see that, according to the *Lao Zi*, the multitude do not have true knowledge, which is possessed by only the few. The few know because they know that they do not know, while the masses do not know but think they know (see Chapter 71). The masses think that they can get more knowledge by actively pursuing it, while the few know that knowledge lies in a profound understanding of human ignorance, which the endless chasing of 'knowledge' can only distract us from. This is why 'the pursuit of learning [human knowledge] is to increase day after day, while the pursuit of the Way is to decrease day after day' (Chapter 48).

> Without going out of the door, one can know the world;
> Without looking out of the window, one can see the Way of
>   Heaven.
> The farther one goes, the less one knows.
> Therefore the sage knows without going here and there,
>   understands without seeing, and accomplishes without action.
>   (Chapter 47; cf. Chapter 52)

The characteristics of the (Daoist) sages discussed above can be summarized as follows:

> Great perfection seems wanting, but its utility will not cease.
> Great fullness seems empty, but its utility will not be exhausted.
> Great straightness seems crooked; great skilfulness seems clumsy;
>   great eloquence seems to stutter.
> … purity and stillness are the model for the world. (Chapter 45)

One might imagine that, although human beings are incompetent and most of us are unaware of our incompetence, we may obtain help from something greater than us. Unfortunately, according to the *Lao Zi*, great nature does not heed the call of human beings. For 'heaven and earth are not humane; they treat the myriad creatures as straw dogs' (Chapter 5).[5] Here, 'not humane' does not mean cruel; rather, heaven and earth have no interest in human beings, no concern one way or the other. The notion that heaven and earth care about human beings is simply what human beings like to believe, and it lacks any basis. It is as if ants believed that human beings care about them so much that they would try to save them. While human beings have the power not to stamp on ants, very few would bother watching where they stepped to avoid an 'ant tragedy'. Conversely, very few, other than perhaps naughty children, would bother to step on ants deliberately in order to kill them.[6] According to the *Lao Zi*, we human beings are too insignificant for heaven and earth, or for great nature, to give us special treatment.

Therefore it is human hubris and ignorance that lead people into believing that they can change the course of nature, either by themselves or by some divine grace. The reason we might want to change the course of nature is our attachment to one side of a pair of opposites. The solution, then, is to look past distinctions and discriminations, or the 'two'. The distinctions will still be there, but they do not drive us to do anything that we human beings are doomed not to be able to do, and no greater power will come to our aid. By dissolving distinctions this way, we will embrace 'the one' (Chapters 10 and 22):

> One who yields will be preserved; something that is bent will become straight; something that is empty will become full; something that is worn out will be renewed; something that has little will gain; something that has plenty will be perplexed.
>
> This is why the sage embraces the one and serves as model for the world…
>
> Because he does not contend, no one in the world can contend with him… (Chapter 22)

When we embrace the one – that is, accept things as they are and not wish for another state – we will stop taking action and instead follow what is natural. As Liu Xiaogan 刘笑敢, a contemporary scholar of Daoism, puts it, '"Naturalness" is the core value of the thought of Laozi [the *Lao Zi*], while *wuwei* [non-action] is the principle or method for realizing this value in action' (Liu 1998: 211). Traditional Chinese philosophy is sometimes accused of advocating quietism. This is a fundamental misunderstanding. As discussed earlier, Confucians are very proactive. But even in the *Lao Zi*, which openly and consistently advocates non-action, it is made clear that we human beings cannot stop taking action. So, 'non-action' should be understood as no un-natural action; hence the proposition is not that human beings stop acting, but that we stop acting unnaturally or humanly.[7]

Therefore, echoing the passage from the Yang Zhu chapter of the *Lie Zi* quoted above, the *Lao Zi* considers the Confucian solution based upon meritocracy and the celebration of human wisdom and virtues to be a temporary fix that has long-term negative effects. For it implicitly encourages more competition (striving to become wise and virtuous; to join 'the great men' and not the 'small men'), which is precisely the root cause of social and political problems. In this vision of the world, the Confucian cure is like the Chinese proverb, 'quenching thirst by drinking poisonous wine'. That is, instead of curing social ills, the Confucian solution actually perpetuates them. The *Lao Zi* states, even protests:

> When the great Way is abandoned, there emerges humanity and
>   righteousness.
> When wisdom and intelligence come forth, there emerges great
>   hypocrisy.
> When the six familial relationships are not in harmony, there
>   emerges [the advocacy of] filial piety and care for children.
> When the state is in turmoil, there emerge loyal ministers.
>   (Chapter 18)

Thus,

> Cut off sageliness, abandon wisdom, and the people will benefit a
>   hundredfold;
> Cut off humanity, abandon righteousness, and the people will
>   return to filial piety and parental care... (Chapter 19)

Naturalness and governing with no actions: distinctively Daoist ideas?

The criticism of Confucianism in these chapters is obviously very strong.[8] Many who have read or studied both the *Lao Zi* and the early Confucian classics come to share the belief of Liu Xiaogan that '[a] reverence for "naturalness" is the most distinguishing characteristic of the Daoist scheme of values and what most clearly separates it from Confucian theory, which extols hard work and striving' (Liu

1998: 211–12). But I consider this belief to be somewhat misleading.[9] For Confucius said, 'If there was a ruler who achieved order by taking no action, it was, perhaps, Shun. What did he do? All he did was to hold himself in a respectful posture and to face due south' (*Analects* 15.5).[10] The Chinese term for 'take no action' in this passage is exactly the same term for 'non-action' used in the *Lao Zi*. In the *Analects* 2.1, 'Confucius said, "A ruler who governs his state by virtue is like the north polar star, which remains in its place while all the other stars revolve around it."' Clearly, this passage also suggests that the ideal ruler should take no action. Thus, on the face of it, the idea that the ideal ruler should take no (unnatural) action does not really distinguish early Confucians from the *Lao Zi*. Indeed, if it is the case that Confucius was the first private teacher, and thus all later thinkers could trace their education back to him, it can be argued that Confucius was the first to introduce the idea of governing on the basis of no action.

Moreover, the early Confucians also based the idea of governing with no action on what is natural. Confucius once wished to remain silent; when a protesting Zi Gong asked the question, if he failed to speak 'what can we little disciples ever learn to pass on to others?' Confucius relied: 'Does Heaven say anything? The four seasons run their course and all things are produced. Does Heaven say anything?' (*Analects* 17.19). This reminds us of the opening line of Chapter 23 of the *Lao Zi*, quoted earlier, which reads: 'To be sparing with words is natural.' In Chapter 30 of the Confucian classic *Doctrine of the Mean*, Confucius is praised for his conformity to the natural order. Under this order, everything is produced and developed without injury or conflict. This is why heaven and earth (nature) are great, and by implication it is why the Confucian way is great.

Therefore, rather than being points of contrast, reverence for naturalness and the idea of non-action are ideas shared by Confucius and the *Lao Zi*. The real distinction between them is, rather, how they understand what is natural. The term 'natural' is deceptive inasmuch as it might be thought to possess a natural (self-evident) meaning, but in fact it means different things to different thinkers. For the *Lao Zi*, what is natural for human beings is to have no material desires beyond the bare necessities, and no desires for human knowledge or virtues. For Confucius, on the other hand, what is natural has a clear Confucian moral undertone, especially in the case of Mencius. Moreover, in the *Lao Zi*, as we saw, heaven and earth are said to be indifferent to human desires. But in some of the early Confucian classics, for example the *Doctrine of the Mean*, the portrayal of heaven and earth is humane and benign.[11] Thus, how the ideas of naturalness and non-action are fleshed out makes all the difference. Furthermore, as we will see, Han Fei Zi the Legalist also advocated naturalness and non-action, although his teachings appear to be somewhat different from those of the *Lao Zi* and of the Confucians.

There is also a subtle difference between the kinds of non-action the *Lao Zi* and Confucius advocate. In the ideal situation, according to the *Analects*, the masses' tendency to become good in a Confucian sense has to be brought out by the best ruler, who takes no action beyond being a moral exemplar for the masses, as the comparison between governing by virtue and the function of the north polar star suggests (*Analects* 2.1). The *Lao Zi*, however, maintains that the natural tendency of human beings can be harmless if it is not provoked by others, ideal rulers included. Thus 'the best [rulers] are those whose existence is [merely] known by the people', while the rulers who are loved and praised by the people – the best rulers according to the Confucian standard – are only second best (*Lao Zi* Chapter 17). As contemporary scholar Philip J. Ivanhoe puts it, the force of the virtue of the ideal Confucian ruler is centripetal, while that of the *Lao Zi* is centrifugal (Ivanhoe 1999: 249–50).

A further difference between the early Confucians and the *Lao Zi* is with regard to the principle of governing with no action. For Confucians, this principle is applicable in the ideal case. But the reality during the SAWS era was clearly far from the ideal. An easy way to address the discrepancy between ideality and reality is to allow, and even to encourage, the superior to take actions. This poses no serious issue for early Confucianism, for it recognizes the importance of the role of the elite; indeed, to have a hierarchy and to let the truly superior rule is what is considered 'natural' by early Confucians. The Lao Zi, though, has difficulty in taking this way out. We have already seen that a fundamental insight of the Lao Zi is that the inadequate nature of human beings means they cannot change things according to their desires. How, then, does the Lao Zi deal with the realistic situations of its day?

The preference of the weak and the 'really' natural cycle

Before we consider this difficult question, let me clear up one point. As discussed earlier, one teaching from the Lao Zi is that we should cease making distinctions and having preferences. Good or bad, strong or weak, all should be the same to the enlightened. But the Lao Zi contains many passages where, rather than ignoring distinctions and preferences, it is suggested that the weak, or what is often looked down upon by the masses, be preferred. Immediately after the statement 'returning is how the Way moves', the line reads 'weakness is the function of the Way' (Chapter 40). Throughout the Lao Zi, images of the weak or of what is commonly looked down upon are celebrated, such as the lowly, the empty, the female, the infant, and so on. But does this not also depend upon making distinctions and encouraging people to prefer one in a pair of opposites to the other? For, in merely reversing the common practice, it still makes distinctions and expresses a preference, which will still lead to competition or contention.

There are two possible reasons for the Lao Zi to celebrate what is commonly considered to be negative. One is relatively simple. The call to embrace the weak might have been meant to serve a 'medicinal' or 'therapeutic' purpose. Human beings tend to prefer the strong, the beautiful, the high, the full, the male (during ancient times), and so on. The emphasis on the superiority of their polar opposites might help rid us of common preferences. When we see the utility of these opposites, we might realize that our 'natural' preferences are not that natural, and thus might cease having an attachment to them.

To consider the second reason, let us go back to the opening statement of Chapter 40 of the *Lao Zi*, 'returning is how the Way moves'. If this is indeed the case, things that go astray will be returned by the Dao to their original (natural) places, and human beings have no need to worry about them. This 'go with the flow' attitude is more likely to be found in the other important early Daoist text, *Zhuang Zi*, the in the *Lao Zi*, although in the former there seems to be no universal principle of eternal return. For the *Lao Zi*, however, although all movements, under the master principle of eternal return, are cyclical, there is nevertheless a preferred cycle. Within this cycle, human perversions (unnatural desires or desires for things beyond the bare necessities) are under control, and do not lead to cycles of violent rises and falls. There remain ups and downs in this cycle, but they are neither violent nor extreme. Human beings are born, mature, age and die, but they are not killed in conflicts caused by greed. They work, but only to get enough food to survive. In this preferred cycle, we are returned to our 'root' condition: an apparent stillness and inactivity, which actually consists of peaceful, smooth and slow cyclical movements – that is, natural action. Thus, the principle of eternal return in Chapter 40 has two dimensions, the descriptive and the normative. Descriptively, all things move in cycles, violent and smooth.[12] But the *Lao Zi* has a moral preference for the smooth cycle, anointing it 'natural' (in a normative sense).

With the message of eternal return thus understood, we can appreciate one meaning of the call to favour the weak in the *Lao Zi*. We are being advised here not to incline towards one of a pair of opposites, but to accept the natural state in which opposites coexist, and still turn into each other. But the eternal turning is no longer violent. This is the state of weakness or the root to which the *Lao Zi* calls us to return: a cycle of smooth or natural development and decline.

Difficulties in returning to the natural cycle

How can we get back to this state of natural cyclical movement that appears to be still? The easy answer is for all human beings to appreciate the reality, and to choose to stay in this natural state of their own free will. But, as we saw in Chapter 20, where the lonely 'I' is compared with the multitude, the *Lao Zi* believes that only a few can see the truth. The contrast between the few and the many is a running theme of the *Lao Zi*.

But can the few enlighten the many? Blinded by their human knowledge and wiles, the masses may react to the teachings of the few by mocking them (Chapter 41) and thus cannot be enlightened. Indeed, the masses' lack of understanding can even be a threat to the Daoist messengers. According to this view, to protect both the unknowing masses and the elite messengers, the former must be kept in the dark, and not be enlightened. As Chapter 36 asserts, 'sharp weapons of the state should not be displayed to the people'. This notion brings to mind the perspective of romantic writers such as Jean-Jacques Rousseau, who claims in his *First Discourse* that the difficulty involved in obtaining knowledge is a protection that nature offers us in the effort to keep human beings in a state of 'happy ignorance', where 'eternal wisdom had placed us', much as a protective mother hides dangerous secrets from her child (Rousseau 1964: 46–7).

The message here also echoes the passage from the *Analects* quoted above, in which Confucius warns that the masses should not be allowed to understand the Way, but only be made to follow it (*Analects* 8.9). It seems that the early Confucians and the early Daoists shared an elitist and hierarchical world-view. Yet a crucial difference is that Confucians believe in the power of human knowledge and human virtue, and maintain that the solution to political problems lies in the elite assuming their social and political responsibilities. The *Lao Zi* does not share this belief. Indeed, consistent with its pessimistic view of the capabilities of the many, the *Lao Zi* seems to consider that the many are not capable of going astray on their own. Rather, it is the few men of cunning and unnatural desires, especially bad rulers, who 'enlighten' the many in the wrong way. This kind of elite is held to be the main cause of the world's ills and thus has to be controlled. Here, then, we see the anti-elitist side of the *Lao Zi* – although it must be said that many readers fail to perceive its elitist message.

How are the many to be kept in a state of innocence, a state which few Daoists choose to return to of their own volition? In Chapter 3 of the *Lao Zi*, it is stated that the Daoist sage *causes* (shi 使) the masses to be without knowledge (cunning) or desires by keeping their hearts vacuous, filling their bellies, weakening their ambitions, and strengthening their bones. A similar teaching is offered in Chapter 65, where those who practise Dao *make* people ignorant (innocent) – that is, free from human (unnatural) knowledge. Interestingly, after discussing how the Daoist sage causes his people to be without knowledge or desire, the concluding remark is: 'By acting without action, all things will be in order' (Chapter 3). In Chapter 57, it is further elaborated that the ruler does not need to do anything but be himself. If he is an enlightened Daoist who takes no action, loves tranquility, engages in no activity and has no desires, then the people will transform themselves. Unlike the Confucian ideal of governing with no actions, the Daoist ideal ruler does not stand as an exemplar for the masses, for he is neither loved nor praised by them, but is merely known (Chapter 17). This is consistent with the anti-elitist facet of the *Lao Zi*. Although, like the Confucians, the *Lao Zi* acknowledges the distinctions between the few and the many, it nevertheless denies the elite any active or even exemplary role in the ideal situation. It is elitism without a visible elite class.

However, as discussed, it seems inevitable that there will be the few who will 'invent the wheel' and corrupt the masses, allowing cunning, deceit and desire to run wild. It is naive to believe that they would willingly exercise Daoist self-restraint, or that a barely known non-active ruler could stop them, when they have already become powerful. To deal with the natural perversion of the natural, the all-too-idealistic proposal of non-action is replaced by one that demands 'small' and non-drastic actions. Chapter 37, having repeated the familiar message that if the Daoist ruler takes no action, all things will transform spontaneously, reads: 'If, after transformation, some people should desire to be active, I would restrain them with simplicity.' In order that restraint not agitate the rest of the public, it should be done unnoticeably by way of 'small' actions; this is only possible when those who desire to be active are as yet at a weak, emerging and easily controllable stage. This lesson is expressed through various metaphors in Chapter 64:

> What remains still is easy to hold.
> What is not yet manifest is easy to plan for.
> What is brittle is easy to crack.
> What is minute is easy to scatter.
> Deal with things before they appear.
> Put things in order before disorder arises.
> A tree as big as a man's embrace grows from a tiny shoot.
> A tower of nine stories begins with a heap of earth.
> The journey of a thousand li starts from where one stands.

Curiously, immediately after these lines, which suggest that actions need to be taken before it is too late, we read: 'He who takes action fails.' The last line of this chapter reads: 'Thus he supports all things in their natural state but does not take any action.' So, presumably, taking small actions in support (fu 輔) of all things is the same as taking no action. However, it should be pointed out that such 'non-action' here seems to be quite different from the kind of non-action suggested in many other chapters of the Lao Zi, some quoted above. Moreover, as is clearly stated in Chapter 37, the action of restraint is taken after the non-action has already been taken, but fails to lead all people to transform themselves. This suggests that the action of restraint is not a non-action. Or, at least, we should understand that there are two kinds of non-action: one, non-action in a more ideal state of affairs, where the ruler does not need to make any effort to curb the desires of the masses, other than being content himself and remaining invisible; and two, non-action in a more realistic state of affairs, where the ruler does need to make a conscious effort to prevent those who dare to act from actually acting.

Yet what if the above measures still fail to curb some members of the misbehaving elite? The *Lao Zi* seems to acknowledge this possibility, proposing the taking not only of small actions, but of drastic ones to rein in the renegades. For example, in Chapter 74, after registering an implicit yet extremely powerful protest against the tyranny of a greedy ruler, 'if the the masses are really not afraid of dying, how can one frighten them by threatening to kill them?', the text continues: 'But if the people are really afraid of dying, and know that we will arrest those who do perverse things, who among them would dare to do them?' Here the text seems to sanction punishment by the state, including execution, of truly[13] perverse people. Moreover, in terms of 'international' relations, although the *Lao Zi* registers a strong and powerful protest against war and offers many cautionary notes (for example, Chapters 30, 31 and 46), it nevertheless explicitly states that one can use force when war is inevitable (Chapter 31).

But the use of these drastic means, albeit rarely, poses serious problems for the *Lao Zi*. In Chapter 74, after sanctioning capital punishment, the text continues: 'To stand in for the executioner in killing people is like standing in for the master carpenter in cutting his lumber. Of those who would thus stand in for the master carpenter in cutting his lumber, few get away without injuring their own hands.' Now, how can the ruler make sure, when he orders killings, either through capital punishment or through war, that he does not 'injure his own hands?' First, to kill justly – 'justly' here in the Daoist sense – means to know what is just. But Chapter 73 asks, 'who knows why Heaven dislikes what it dislikes?'[14] Second, even if we know what justice is, much of the *Lao Zi* is trying to teach human beings that we are unable to sustain any unnatural actions, killings being, obviously, in this category. Third, even if we know what is just and are able to fulfil it, another important lesson of the *Lao Zi* seems to be that we do not need to. For 'Heaven's net is indeed vast … it misses nothing' (Chapter 73). Thus the lesson is that one should dare not to dare to take any actions (Chapter 73).

However, if this is the case, what can be the justification for people to punish other people with death? This is one reason the *Lao Zi* registers a strong protest against wars. A passage in Chapter 46 reads:

> When the world has the Way, galloping horses are turned back to fertilize [the fields with their dung; the Chinese word *fen* 糞 can also be translated as 'to farm']; when the world is without the Way, war horses are raised in the suburbs.

The *Lao Zi* sees wars as the harbinger of disasters. In Chapter 30, it observes: 'Wherever an army resides, thorns and thistles grow. In the wake of a large campaign, bad harvests are sure to follow.' It also warns, in Chapter 31, that 'fine weapons are inauspicious instruments', and that even if one wins the war, it should be mourned with funeral rites. In contrast to the early Confucians, the *Lao Zi* seems to believe that no wars are really just. We punish the bad, but this action will create more conflict. Even in a 'just' war ('just' in the common sense), innocent (and not-so-innocent) lives will be lost, and loved ones will hold a grudge that will come back to haunt the 'just' winners. After all, according to the *Lao Zi*, the world functions in a mystical way, beyond our understanding and our control.

In Chapters 30 and 31, the *Lao Zi* advocates caution in the resort to war. But even this cautionary and rare instance already poses a serious challenge to the overall message of the book. Unfortunately, as discussed earlier, the collapse of the old order brought about an age of endless wars by order-less (and ruthless) people, which was the time the *Lao Zi* was written or compiled. The already problematic drastic means of war would have to be deployed often. Moreover, in order to achieve the effect of scaring people into observing 'natural' behaviour, such recourse must be displayed to the public, which is contrary to the teachings of Chapter 36 of the *Lao Zi*, where the frequent use of the sharp weapons of the state and the public display of this use are forbidden.

The ultimate answer: return to small and isolated states with few people

With the aforementioned fundamental problems in mind, let us consider Chapter 80 of the *Lao Zi* in its entirety:

> [Let] there be a small state with few people.
> Let there be ten times and a hundred times as many utensils, but let them not be used.
> Let the people take dying seriously and not migrate far.
> Even if there are ships and carriages, none will ride in them.
> Even if there are armour and weapons, none will display them.
> Let the people again keep their records with knotted string.
> Let them relish their food, beautify their clothing, be content with their homes, and delight in their customs.
> Though neighbouring states are within eyesight and crowing of cocks and barking of dogs can be heard,
> Yet the people there may grow old and die without ever visiting one another.

It might be considered that this chapter attests to the recognition by the *Lao Zi* that its political teaching of governing by non-action, even with the caveat that small actions and limited large actions are permissible, is not possible in large, populous and well-connected states, the new reality of the Chinese world during the SAWS. For this teaching to be apposite, the state must be small in both size and population. Yet the Chinese world at that time already had a relatively large population; and so the solution offered here is that this world should be divided into many small states that do not communicate with each other. Communication is not needed because each state is self-sufficient. Furthermore, although written language is not completely abandoned, it is to be returned to a very primitive stage of using knotted string. Likewise, the Chinese world already possessed advanced technologies; so in these small states they would be left unused, and stood to be forgotten in time. The technologies for communication and transportation between states would find no use in these small and isolated states, and the lack of a sophisticated written language would further help their disappearance. Technologies of use only in a well-connected and large state also would find no utility, and probably could not be invented or maintained in a small state. Moreover, since each state described in Chapter 80 is small in terms of its size and population, the centralization of a large amount of wealth becomes extremely difficult. Such concentration is the key to technological advance and increase in demand, for if great wealth is monopolized in the hands of the few, unimaginable luxuries will be desired by people within a society of relative equality; that is, by setting an example, the rich will fuel material desires among all. This will further lead to fierce competition and social unrest. Furthermore, the concentration of wealth is often a necessary condition for great technological advance and social projects that will lead to a further concentration of wealth and increased technological advance. Besides, the lack of sophisticated written language in these small states will ensure accidental advances are likely to be forgotten in the next generation.

The late American scholar of China Benjamin Schwartz is one of the few who understood the significance of Chapter 80 to the overall political philosophy of the *Lao Zi*. After quoting this chapter in full, he writes:

> This does not seem to be the description of a utopia of the prime-val past. Clearly we are in a period when 'advanced technology' is available. The sage-ruler, however, sees to it (lit. 'causes' *shih*) that it is rejected. The sage realizes that the complexity of the civiliza-tion is to some extent the function of size; therefore, he prescribes a 'small community.' What the language suggests is not a spontane-ously emerging 'anarchist' state, but a state of affairs brought about by a sage-ruler. (Schwartz 1985: 212–13)

As we have seen, the new reality of the Chinese world during the SAWS was the emergence of large, populous and well-connected

states. Perhaps the authors of the *Lao Zi* realized that all manner of
new social ills would become inevitable in this kind of world. Driven
by new-found riches, luxuries and other desirables made possible by
a well-connected and large society, people will engage in fierce competition for these prizes. As a consequence, people's morals become
corrupted; deceit, crime and killings run wild. The pristine natural
state where people are governed with no unnatural actions cannot
be achieved in this new world. Thus, instead of embracing the brave
new world or the world of modernity, as early Confucians did, the
authors of the *Lao Zi* wanted the world to return to pre-modern times.
Yes, there would be fewer material goods, and much of 'civilization'
with its sophisticated written language would be lost, and perhaps
even relapse into ignorance, but compared to the perceived evils in
the new world this would be a price worth paying.

Such an understanding of modernity, along with associated reactions, can be found in the Romantic thinkers of the West during
the period of Western modernization. In his *Second Discourse*, Rousseau
posits a hypothetical state of nature which existed even before human
civil society emerged.[15] In the state of nature, the life of the savage
man is solitary and effortlessly self-sufficient. He is indolent and
content, subject to few passions, and possesses sentiment and intellect
suited to that state. He has no company and no need of his fellow
men, and has no means (language) to communicate with them even
if they are together. Given the savage man's lack of both intelligence
and desires, no inventions are likely to be forthcoming. Even if they
were, they would perish with him without being communicated
to others, 'because he [the savage man] did not recognize even his
children' (Rousseau 1964: 137). In such a state, with no one, or few,
to emulate and lacking even the means to communicate, which is the
precondition for spreading tales of exotic lands, and with no desirable
objects or conditions, the excessive desires of the savage man could
not be aroused; in the case of sexual desire, 'any woman is good
for him' (135). Thus, if a human being could be put in this solitary
state with no advanced means of communication, according to the

Lao Zi, all the social ills and evils consequent upon the deviation of human beings from the natural state of innocence (lacking human knowledge) and absence of rampant desires would not arise.

In this hypothetical state, however, there are only solitary savage men, and not small and isolated states, as suggested in the *Lao Zi*. The civilizations in these states seem to be already too advanced for Rousseau. For example, they have a spoken and a primitive written language. According to Rousseau, the invention of language was a miraculous accident, which he sees as pivotal to the fall of human beings from the stage of savages to that of civilized society ridden with evils (Rousseau 1964: 119–22). Nevertheless, he himself suggests that society is not necessarily bad. Indeed, at the dawning of society, with its form of family settlements, society maintains 'a golden mean between the indolence of the primitive state and the petulant activity of our vanity' (150–52). This stage 'must have been the happiest and most durable epoch', and man 'must have come out of it by some fatal accident, which for the common good ought never have happened' (151). The culprits in this fatal development are agriculture and metallurgy. Compared to this ideal society, the small states described in Chapter 80 of the *Lao Zi* are already on their way down the road of no return, since they have not only a language, but very likely agriculture and metallurgy as well. However, for Rousseau, language, agriculture and metallurgy are bad because they promote rationality, communication and dependence, all of which might have been effectively curtailed in the small states described in the *Lao Zi*. Moreover, even Rousseau realizes that it is hopeless, too radical, to go back to that perfect stage, once human beings have been cursed with those fatal developments (Rousseau 1964: 201–3). Indeed, his moderate solution, as suggested by the dedication of his *Second Discourse* 'To the Republic of Geneva', is precisely a small state with a small population. Such a state is not so rich as to be able to develop luxuries that will corrupt 'solid virtues', but is not so poor as to be incapable of self-sufficiency (84). Such a small state, like the one in the *Lao Zi*, resembles a scaled-up savage man. Of course, Rousseau's central concern is the protection of freedom and equality; hence another crucial justification for the small size of his ideal state is that it has to consist of citizens who have, like loving friends, one and the same interest, so as to form a true republic based upon active citizenship (78–9). These features are not present in the small state of the Lao Zi. As mentioned in Chapter 1, in spite of the many profound similarities, there are significant differences between Chinese early modernity and the European phase. Importantly, the Europeans possessed the cultural heritage of Ancient Greece and Rome. Rousseau's concern with freedom, equality and other republican virtues, absent from the Lao Zi, may owe a great deal to this unique European cultural legacy.

The insight of the Lao Zi and Rousseau regarding the connection between the complexity of civilization and the size and population of the state seems to be borne out by empirical studies. In Jared Diamond's fascinating work Guns, Germs, and Steel, he concludes, having studied the peoples on a number of isolated islands, that

> Human populations of only a few hundred people were unable to survive indefinitely in complete isolation. A population of 4,000 were able to survive for 10,000 years, but with significant cultural losses and significant failures to invent, leaving it with a uniquely simplified material culture. (Diamond 1999: 313)

His example of the Tasmanians is especially striking (312). A population of 4,000, they had lost the techniques and tools for fishing, along with awls, needles and other bone implements. In addition, they were unable to invent independently, or had lost, many other very basic tools.

Yet it must also be registered that many other arguments offered by the Lao Zi and Rousseau have not fared so well empirically. The hypothesis that human beings started out as solitary savage men accounts for the fact that Rousseau found the invention of language so miraculous. But this hypothesis is empirically dubious, because it is very likely that human beings have always lived in groups. Empirical studies also show that the Lao Zi's and Rousseau's romantic understanding of the peaceful primitive life is highly problematic, particularly in view of the fact that the state exists largely as an effective means to reduce violence.[16] Of course, Rousseau's account of the 'state of nature', like the *Lao Zi*'s account of the ideal state, is not empirical, but normative. Nevertheless the challenge from empirical studies at least casts doubt on their *constructive* projects *as a whole*.[17] This challenge remains relevant today, because the views of many 'humanists' of a romantic bent (for example, the hippies in the 1960s and those in the contemporary world who idealize Tibet as a Shangri-La, a heaven-on-earth) and individualists resonate with the ideas of Rousseau and the *Lao Zi*.

Can we bring about 'small states with few people'?

There is a final puzzle to solve in our understanding of the political philosophy of the *Lao Zi*. Suppose for argument's sake we acknowledge its desirability, how could we go back to the stage of 'small states with few people'? The Tasmanians returned to the state of 'innocence' because their connection to other groups was cut off by the rising sea and they did not have appropriate watercraft (Diamond 1999: 312). But the *Lao Zi*, as a work of political philosophy, needs to offer something less arbitrary than the entreaty 'let the sea level rise!' As we noted above, Schwartz suggests that this return is brought about by a sage ruler. But such an action would have to be heroic and drastic, assuming that the sage-ruler could somehow – and it would take nothing short of a miracle – obtain the power to lead such an action. Another possibility is that, following an extremely violent phase, the huge and populous state may spontaneously collapse into several sparsely populated small states because the deviants would kill each other off, and advances lethal to the existence of the small state would be destroyed in the wake of the disintegration. Then, with the conscious effort of each state's sage ruler, or on the part of an overlord of all these states, the preferred cycle would be maintained indefinitely. After all, as we saw, the *Lao Zi* maintains that anything violent and drastic – that is, unnatural – won't last long. Moreover, in a commentary on the first four lines of Chapter 36, where the *Lao Zi* offers four tactics of the 'subtle light', among them the observation 'In order to destroy, it is necessary first to promote', Wang Bi writes: 'If you want to get rid of the strong and the violent, you have to use these four [tactics]. You follow the nature of things, destroying them by making them kill themselves, not by using punishments or being the strongest. This is indeed a subtle light' (Wang Bi 1991: 21). The suggestion here seems to be that when the world is already in turmoil a sage should 'lay low', waiting for great Nature to do away with the violent and the strong. This will occur on account of the universal and descriptive principle of 'returning is how the Dao moves'. Then, once the strong and violent have destroyed themselves, the sage should help to maintain the primitive state that emerges from the chaos, sometimes by taking small actions, less frequently by taking larger ones. The development of such a state will be part of the preferred and normative cycle of 'natural' movement.

The last step of this big 'conspiracy' is partially described in the classical He Shang Gong 河上公 commentary, which is believed to be close to the Huang-Lao tradition that is focused on the political teachings of the *Lao Zi*. The title that this commentary gives to Chapter 80, which is meant to sum up the gist of this chapter, can be understood and translated as 'Independence', 'Standing alone' or 'Self-sufficiency' (*duli* 独立). The commentary on the very first line reads:

> Even though the sages govern a large state, it is as though it were small. Being frugal they do not demand too much. Even though the people are numerous, it is as though they were few. The sage would not think of wearing them out.[18]

To an extent, this 'conspiracy' did occur in Chinese history. After seemingly endless wars and conquests during the Warring States era, the most powerful and brutal state, Qin, emerged victorious. It unified the Chinese world by using all the sharp weapons of the state;

yet this use might have contributed to its early demise. The first few Han rulers that came after the Qin dynasty are said to have followed the teaching of Huang-Lao, and adopted the policy of reducing the government's role over people's lives (yuminxiuxi 与民休息, 'allowing the people to rest'). The return to such a policy has often been adopted after a violent phase of dynastic transition.

However, the success of the teachings of the Lao Zi is limited at best. For the Chinese dynasties following the Qin dynasty weren't able to stay for very long in the stage of de facto isolated small states with few people. Connections between villages were re-established, wealth was gradually accumulated in the hands of the few, inequality became intolerable, and finally devastating revolts broke out. We can argue that this was because the so-called de facto small states with few people are not really any such thing. They were unified under a centralized government that, at times, treated the whole empire as if it consisted of small states with few people. But for this stage to last, 'as if' was not enough. For, once people start to become aware of the outside world, unless something really drastic happens (like the rise in sea level for the Tasmanians), the best the Daoist can hope for is this 'as if' stage, which, however, cannot last for long.

The contemporary world is even more troublesome to the Daoists. As the contemporary scholar D.C. Lau points out,

> If the Taoist [Daoist] philosopher could have visited our society, there is no doubt that he would have considered popular education and mass advertising the twin banes of modern life. The one causes the people to fall from their original state of innocent ignorance; the other creates new desires for objects no one would have missed if they had not been invented. (Lau 1963: xxxi)

Thus, the only hope that the teachings of the Lao Zi could be adopted comprehensively and constructively lies in the expectation of some apocalyptic occurrence. That is, perhaps human desires will drive us to the point of total destruction, after which we will be returned to a primitive stage of small states with few people (or even no people), fulfilling the *Lao Zi*'s universal and descriptive principle of the 'eternal return'. But it seems doubtful that many people would pin their hopes on this outcome.

With the difficulties of the political proposal in the *Lao Zi* clarified, we may be able to appreciate the political insight of the *Zhuang Zi*. The existence of the Daoist philosopher Zhuang Zi 庄子 is far less controversial than Lao Zi. He probably lived during the Warring States period, and is said to have written the book *Zhuang Zi*. But whether in fact he wrote the entire book is a controversial issue. The common view is that many chapters, especially the so-called 'outer' and 'mixed' chapters, were written by his followers, or even others, while the inner chapters were written by him. There are passages in the *Zhuang Zi* whose ideas echo those found in the Yang Zhu chapter in the *Lie Zi* and in the *Lao Zi*. There are many amusing and fanciful stories and counter-intuitive insights on life in the *Zhuang Zi*, which make it a fascinating read. Together with ideas from the *Lao Zi*, these tales and insights offered comfort to those traditional Chinese intellectuals who failed to realize their political ambitions. After all, it is comforting to learn that, for example, even if one's political ambitions are realized, such are considered by great nature to be merely a laughing matter – a notion often expressed in the aphorisms in the *Lao Zi* and in the sardonic and playful stories in the *Zhuang Zi*. This and other ideas from the *Zhuang Zi* constitute part of the psyche of traditional Chinese intellectuals, especially the artistic among them. But, other than constituting background culture, the *Zhuang Zi* does not seem to have a place in political philosophy. However, the strong apolitical attitude found in the *Zhuang Zi* may have reflected a great political insight. As Schwartz points out, Zhuang Zi understood the difficulties in the teachings of the *Lao Zi*, and therefore dropped the 'primitivist' critique of civilization completely, replacing it with an 'all-enveloping historical fatalism' (Schwartz 1985: 188, 229–33). In other words, the *Zhuang Zi* depoliticizes the *Lao Zi*, though it is, nonetheless, based upon a political insight. Perhaps for the author(s) of the *Zhuang Zi* the world was too chaotic for any universal principle to work, such as 'Returning is how the Way (Dao) moves', and thus it offers none, unlike the *Lao Zi*.

A story in the *Zhuang Zi* beautifully illustrates the arbitrariness of its times. A tree is saved from being cut down on the grounds that it is useless (its timber is good for nothing), and a goose is killed because it is useless (it cannot cackle). When asked which side he comes down on, Zhuang Zi claims that even settling for midway between being useful and being useless is no good because it is still driven by the concern with use, and thr right choice is to roam free with the Dao (Way) (*Zhuang Zi* Chapter 20).[19]

For the *Zhuang Zi*, then, no rational principles are applicable to this world; and it does not bother to offer any serious political solution to the problems of its times because it considers them to be unsolvable. It focuses instead on how the Daoist elite can obtain happiness by avoiding the hopeless world and enjoying individual freedom by way of Zhuangzian 'enlightenment'. Clearly, it is far easier to follow the teachings of the *Lao Zi* in one's private and personal life; that is, in Zhuang Zi's apolitical way. After all, an individual is able to 'lay low' and avoid proximity to the deviants of the world, whereas for the ruler of a large, populous and well-connected state contact with them is inevitable.

Lessons for today

The two texts discussed in this chapter, the *Lao Zi* and the *Zhuang Zi*, have been influential in Chinese history, especially among the educated elite. Nowadays they are often read as an antidote to rampant commercialism and the naked pursuit of worldly desires. As we have seen, the books do address this dimension. In the modern world, once in a while the call to return to a simpler life becomes popular; the most recent occasion being the financial crisis of 2008 and the 'great recession' that has followed. These two texts echo this call, and those who wish to return to a simpler life may find insights in them. However, as discussed in this chapter, those who hold out hope for the masses to return to a pristine life, with no complicating institutional arrangements ('small and isolated states with few people'), are destined to be disappointed. For example, it was hoped that the financial crisis would provide shock therapy to the commercialism of the contemporary world, and for a moment people did appear to save more, work harder and consume less. But as soon as we feel we are emerging from the deepest hole we have yet dug, we resume our 'normal' ways of consumption in the populous, interconnected and advanced world in which we live. The insights from the *Lao Zi*, then, offer both inspiration and caution to today's 'romantics'.

The *Lao Zi* and the *Zhuang Zi* have also been read as critiques of Confucian political teachings. As we have seen in this chapter, many of the criticisms they offer are indeed incisive. Even if one insists on the superiority of the Confucian teachings, one is obliged to take seriously and address the critique they advance. However, I consider the *Lao Zi* to be more than a mere objection to Confucianism, as it contains a constructive political dimension of its own, which has played a notable role in Chinese political history. Nevertheless its political proposal has some fundamental problems. Be that as it may, certain key insights of the *Lao Zi* are subsequently picked up by Han Fei Zi in the Warring States period, as we will see, and even find an echo in currents of modern European economic and political thought that still exert influence today. Thus, let us now turn to another response to Chinese modernity: Legalism.

FIVE

The Legalists: builders of
modern bureaucracy and institutions

Having discussed early Confucianism and Daoism, we now turn to
the last school of traditional Chinese thought that will be examined,
Legalism. As we have seen, in response to issues brought to the
fore by China's early modernity, early Daoists simply rejected the
development, and yearned to return to a pre-modern stage; although
this stage was not really the feudal system. The early Confucians, for
their part, ostensibly argued for a return to the feudal system; some
of them might have sincerely wished for it. But they reinterpreted
the old system, and these reinterpretations actually addressed new
issues. So, consciously or unconsciously, they embraced modernity
and were committed to moving on. As this chapter will show,
the so-called Legalists, in contrast, consciously and unabashedly
embraced modernity, and did not even bother to hide their embrace
behind a conservative facade, as the Confucians did. They were the
builders of modern bureaucracy and established institutions that laid
the foundation for Chinese traditional political regimes for the next
two thousand years. In this chapter, by looking at two important
Legalists, Shang Yang and Han Fei Zi, we will see how they built
this modern bureaucracy in theory and in practice. In this work, they
(especially Han Fei Zi) were also ferocious critics of the Confucian

response to modernity. Interestingly, we will also see that Han Fei Zi seems to be inspired by some of the teachings in the *Lao Zi*. In this chapter, then, we will see an interplay among the three schools of traditional Chinese political philosophy. As in the previous chapters, I will also show how Legalist ideas resonate with some modern European thinking, and how comparisons and contrasts between them also serve to shed light on contemporary issues.

The Chinese term for the Legalist school is *fa jia* 法家, or the school of *fa*. *Fa* can mean laws, rules and regulations, principles, methods, measures, and the like. Thus the translation 'Legalism' can be misleading because it focuses on merely one aspect of the Chinese term *fa*. Moreover, as in the case of most schools of thought in human history, whether those we know as Legalist thinkers considered themselves to belong to this school and whether those proclaimed as belonging to it do in fact share certain core ideas are controversial issues.[1] The extant works of most of those labelled 'Legalists' are fragmentary at best, and the records of their lives and deeds are somewhat sketchy. The two exceptions are Shang Yang 商鞅, also known as Lord Shang, and Han Fei Zi 韩非子. A book titled *The Book of Lord Shang* 商君书 is still available, but its authenticity (i.e. whether it was written by Lord Shang or is a reliable source of his ideas) is seriously doubted. But we do know a relatively large amount about the life of Lord Shang. With regard to the second thinker, although some chapters and passages in the *Han Fei Zi* are of doubtful provenance, much of the work is considered to have been written by the historical Han Fei Zi. We also know a good deal about his life. As Lord Shang and Han Fei Zi are the two most influential Legalists in Chinese history, it is appropriate that I focus here on the lives and thoughts of these two men.

The life and deeds of Legalist Shang Yang

An entire volume (Volume 68) of the *Shiji* is dedicated to the life of Shang Yang (c. 395–338 BCE) (Sima 1981: 254–6). According to this record, his original name was Gongsun Yang 公孙鞅. He was of noble pedigree, the origin of which can be traced back to a ruler of the feudal state Wei 卫, a very weak state during the Warring States period. This accounts for the fact that Shang Yang is also known as Wei Yang. When he was young, he enjoyed the teachings of early Legalists, and served the prime minister of Wei 魏, which was one of the seven strongest states during the Warring States period and not to be confused with Shang Yang's ancestral state. This prime minister was dying before he was able to appoint Shang Yang to any significant position. Greatly appreciating his talent, the prime minister recommended him to the king, asking the king to entrust him with state affairs, adding that if the king did not want to do this, then he should kill him to prevent him from being employed by another state. The king chose neither of these options, thinking that his prime minister must have been confused, so close to death. Shang Yang then went to the state of Qin. There he tried to have the ear of the king, but the king did not appreciate his speech with its talk of the Kingly Way (wang dao 王道), which is likely close to the Confucian notion of ideal rulership. Finally, he got the ear of the king by offering advice on how to make the state strong (rather than humane, which would be the Confucians' preferred focus). Later, he was enfeoffed at a place called Shang, hence he was subsequently known as Shang Yang or Lord Shang, after he led the Qin army to defeat Wei, the state that he once served.

With the king's blessing, Shang Yang introduced his radical reforms in Qin. Instead of sticking to or reviving the old feudal system, he established and developed policies and rules (fa) that would become the legacy for traditional Chinese regimes to come. He advocated the centralization of power. Instead of the pyramid-like feudal system in which the monarch rules directly over princes of various ranks (duke, earl, etc.), while each fiefdom has its autonomy, Shang Yang helped Qin to develop what would later become the so-called jun xian 郡县 system; that is, the king would appoint officials at every level, from provinces (jun) to counties (xian). He also helped to unify standards of measurement. He promoted the authority of a unified system of laws and rules, and at the same time suppressed different schools of thought. Along with this strengthening of centralized power, he also tried to suppress elements that might help form cliques threatening the centralized power. He addressed the political issue of the conflict between private and public by characterizing it as one between a centralized state and various elements able to form alternative, decentralized power bases. He grouped a few families together, and made sure that each family would watch over other families to detect potential crimes against the state, rewarding those who turned others in (in contrast to the Confucian notion of mutual concealment) and punishing those who failed to do so. Indeed, under this system, if one family committed a crime, all the others would be punished too. Shang Yang also encouraged the 'nuclear family' by heavily taxing families with two or more adult brothers still living together – as presumably big families could form power centres that might threaten the rule of the state (another policy that Confucians would strongly oppose) and dividing big families into smaller units could encourage people to venture into new farmland. He also punished severely those who dared to 'take matters into their own hands', such as swordsmen for hire or those who meted out 'street justice'. In his world-view, it was essential for the state to have the monopoly on violence.

Shang Yang promoted policies that weakened the power of the traditional nobility, perceived as a potential threat to centralized power, abolishing many of their privileges. For example, inheritance of noble titles was made contingent on military achievement, and laws from which the nobility were previously exempt would now apply equally to them. More importantly, instead of maintaining the feudal system, in which the nobility inherited land, he established policies that acknowledged private ownership and allowed land to be freely sold.

These reforms were linked to another set of policies introduced by Lord Shang. For him, what made a state strong was farming and military achievements. So he devised various policies that encouraged these activities. For instance, he established a meritocracy based upon military achievements, rather than upon either inherited nobility or Confucian virtues and wisdom. The free sale of land encouraged a strong work ethic in farming. At the same time, he attempted to suppress commerce, in line with the belief that it did not really create wealth for the state and discouraged hard work among the masses.

Shang Yang's radical reforms needed credibility. To achieve this, according to one anecdote, he once put a beam outside a gate of the capital, stating that the man who moved the beam inside the gate would be rewarded handsomely, for what seemed to be a rather simple task. People considered this ridiculous and so no one took up the challenge. He then increased the award fourfold. Someone eventually fulfilled the task and was duly rewarded. This helped establish the credibility of his future policies. Many people found the new policies inconvenient. Even the crown prince violated one of the new laws. He could not be brought to book, however, and so Shang Yang instead punished his teacher. He also sent those who dared to challenge his new policies into exile. Such draconian methods further strengthened the credibility of his new policies.

After the king died, the new king and the nobles who had been ill-treated by Shang Yang finally got their chance for revenge. He escaped to the border, but the innkeeper there, not knowing who he was, refused to let him stay, saying that, according to the rules laid down by Lord Shang, someone with no identity could not be taken in. Finally, he returned to his own fiefdom. However, he and his followers were defeated by the Qin army, and he was brutally killed.

The irony of Shang Yang's fate gave those who objected to his draconian laws and policies, such as the Confucians, a degree of comfort and even pleasure, because his death seemed to mark the limitation of his political proposals (his failure to escape punishment under the draconian laws). But the fact that even a powerful person like him could not escape punishment under the laws he helped establish actually showed the power of his policies. In spite of reaction on the part of the new king and the nobles, the reforms remained intact, enabling Qin to become the most powerful state of them all, and finally leading to the unifying of China. As indicated, the policies and institutions established by Shang Yang were to lay the foundation of political regimes in China for two millennia. Many of these policies bear comparison with reforms introduced during the phase of European modernization.

The life of Han Fei Zi

In terms of practical achievement, Shang Yang is arguably the most influential Legalist thinker. In the realm of theory, though, the most influential Legalist is Han Fei Zi (c. 281–233 BCE). As we have seen, the overall authenticity of the book *Han Fei Zi* is less open to question than that of the *Book of Lord Shang*. More importantly, the *Han Fei Zi* contains a more synthetic, profound and coherent theoretical system that supersedes that in the *Book of Lord Shang*. Thus, whereas I have discussed only the life and practical reform programme of Lord Shang, I will focus on both Han Fei Zi the person and *Han Fei Zi* the book.

The following account of Han Fei Zi's life is, again, from *Shiji*, in which there is a volume devoted to Lao Zi, Zhuang Zi, Han Fei Zi and another thinker, Shen Buhai 申不害, who is often categorized as a Legalist (Volume 63; Sima 1981: 247–8). Han Fei Zi was a prince, a member of the extended ruling family of the State of Han, one of the seven strong states during the Warring States period, albeit one of the weaker ones, perhaps even the weakest. His obsession was to prevent his home state being annexed by other states, especially the State of Qin. The opening two chapters of the *Han Fei Zi* are an explicit call for Qin not to annex Han. Apparently, he never had the ear of the king in the State of Han; the consequent sense of frustration and thwarted ambition might account for his producing so many political writings, which only later were edited into a single book. Ironically, he eventually managed to gain the ear of the king – not the ear of the king of Han but that of the king of Qin, he who would later conquer all the other strong states, unify China and become 'First Emperor' of the Qin dynasty. After reading the work of Han Fei Zi, the king of Qin waged a war against the former's home state, in the cause of having him in his company. The state of Han, being defeated, sent Han Fei Zi to Qin. Li Si 李斯, who studied with Han Fei Zi under the Confucian Xun Zi and who informed the king of Qin that the works he so admired were by his former classmate Han Fei, nevertheless felt threatened by Han Fei's presence at the Qin court. So, together with another person who shared this sense of threat, he talked the king into forcing Han Fei Zi to commit suicide. The king regretted his action only when it was too late.

As with Shang Yang, Han Fei Zi's death is not without irony. The argument that Li Si used to persuade the king to kill Han Fei Zi was not 'Legalistic' but rather Confucian in tenor. He argued that Han Fei Zi was a prince of the state of Han, and that it is only human (and natural) that in a war for domination Han Fei Zi would always make common cause with the state of Han. It seems that Li Si did not believe, as Han Fei Zi argued in his book, that people's loyalty can be earned through the use of rewards and punishments. It should be added that Li Si himself did not fare much better: he was brutally executed by the Second Emperor of Qin.

A further irony relating to Han Fei Zi is that, although his teachings were often condemned by later scholars and politicians, his book has nevertheless long been popular – celebrated not for its political thinking, but for its beautiful prose and often amusing stories. Paradoxically, perhaps, this master writer and lobbyist was said to be someone who stuttered.

Moreover, two chapters of the *Han Fei Zi* address the difficulty experienced by a truly loyal and thoughtful subject in gaining the ear of the king (Chapters 3 and 12). Han Fei Zi argues that those close to the king are in reality self-serving and disloyal, and will do anything and everything in their power to obstruct the truly loyal and thoughtful subject, including having him killed. It is likely that these people will prevail. Of course Han Fei Zi himself tried to gain the king's ear (first the king of Han and then the king of Qin), only to get himself killed for his trouble. His fate led later commentators to observe that his actions failed to follow his own awareness and understanding (Chen 2000: 1226, 1257). But his tragic death may merely have been testament to the extreme difficulty of gaining the king's ear, which, under certain circumstances, proved too much even for the ability of a master of this art (1228). Generally speaking, the failure of an individual to follow his or her own philosophy, ironic as it is, does not invalidate that philosophy.

Another irony associated with Legalism is that although, following Shang Yang's policies and other reforms of which Han Fei Zi would approve, the state of Qin unified China, the Qin dynasty (221–206 BCE) was nevertheless itself overturned only fifteen years after its founding. This apparent paradox was grist to the mill for Confucians and others: it further demonstrated to those who abhorred Legalist teachings the limitations of the school's political philosophy. Yet, as I have already argued, the supposed ironies and inconsistencies associated with Legalist thinkers and practitioners do not discredit Legalist philosophy as such. As for the fate of Qin, one reason for its early demise may have been that the political changes the Qin dynasty brought about were simply too drastic for the country to accommodate in such a short period of time. And so the 'tyrannical Qin' (baoqin 暴秦) – a term its critics liked to use – was overturned shortly after its founding and replaced by the Han dynasty. The Han first tried to go back to the 'good old ways' of the feudal system, only to encounter trouble itself early on: the revolt of the seven kings (qi wang zhi luan 七王之乱). It eventually went back to the political system, with some revisions, of the Qin dynasty, an order that contained many arrangements suggested in the Han Fei Zi. This system would largely be followed throughout subsequent Chinese history.

Han Fei Zi: the successor to the Lao Zi on natural laws

Before we come to the discussion of the Han Fei Zi, let me be clear about how this book is read here. The first point to note, as discussed in the Introduction, is that the early Chinese classics were not written in the form of treatises; the system of thought has to be explicated by the reader. Naturally, this process will generate controversies. The *Han Fei Zi* in fact contains far more extensive argumentation than many other classics of the time; nevertheless an understanding of its system still demands interpretation from the reader. Second, the *Han Fei Zi* is often read as a book of political legerdemain. It cannot be denied that it does contain much shameless practical advice to politicians of different ranks – or at least many passages can be read as suggestive of the dark arts. The *Lao Zi* is also sometimes read as such, and some even read it as a guidebook of sexual practices that will serve to prolong life. But I will read the book of *Han Fei Zi* as having been written according to an underlying system of political theory – a theory I will attempt to illustrate. If this reading is successful, the reader will see that the book does indeed possess a theoretical dimension.

As we have seen, in *Shiji* the biography of Han Fei Zi is put together with that of Lao Zi, which suggests that Sima Qian, one of the greatest Chinese historians, had good reason to think of the works of the two thinkers as directly comparable. Indeed, Sima Qian explicitly states that Han Fei Zi's thoughts are based upon some basic ideas of Lao Zi's, although the latter's philosophy is far more profound (Sima 1981: 248). Han Fei Zi was often extremely critical, and in brutally caustic terms, of many other authoritative schools during the SAWS, but he never targeted the *Lao Zi*. In fact, there are phrases and ideas throughout the *Han Fei Zi* that allude to material in the *Lao Zi*. Indeed, Chapters 20 and 21 of the *Han Fei Zi* are actually devoted to interpreting and illustrating passages of the *Lao Zi*. This has puzzled many readers. For whereas the *Lao Zi* is usually understood as rejecting active governmental control, against the frequent use of punishment, and opposed to war and conquest, these policies and practices are precisely what the *Han Fei Zi* is understood to advocate strongly. For example, a line from the *Lao Zi* reads: 'The more laws and edicts are made prominent, the more thieves and robbers there will be' (Chapter 57),[2] while, as we will see, Han Fei Zi wanted laws and edicts to be well known and strictly followed by the masses. As the previous chapter showed, the Lao Zi found modernity problematic, and wished for society to go back to a pristine, pre-modern stage. Han Fei Zi, for his part, as we will see in this chapter, staunchly embraced modernity, and was critical of those, such as early Confucians, who, in his view, failed to understand that one can never go back to the good old days and the political institutions of yesterday.

In spite of all these apparent differences, Han Fei Zi found a kindred spirit in the Lao Zi. Of course, the text of the Lao Zi – if indeed one can speak of a single text, with or without this title – to which Han Fei Zi had access might have been quite different from that which we have today, and facilitated a far more straightforward reading. For want of a more reliable historical record, let us put this possibility aside and instead search for resonances in these two texts. A key insight of the Lao Zi is that, compared with the great Dao or Way, human wisdom and ability are as nothing. By not obeying the Way, we can only achieve self-destruction. Moreover, nature would not bother to change its ways for pathetic beings like us. As we have seen, Han Fei Zi's teacher Xun Zi the Confucian also believed in the separation between the heavenly way and the human way, but like other Confucians he believed it possible for human beings to improve the world in which they live. Siding with the Lao Zi and sharply at odds with the Confucians, Han Fei Zi thought that we human beings are powerless against the Dao. Therefore, instead of acting humanly, we should follow the Way, and play no active (unnatural or un-Way-like) role in politics.

Implicit in the Lao Zi and explicit in the Han Fei Zi is the idea that the Way can be understood as the natural laws of politics, among other meanings. For the Lao Zi, these laws dictate that in a large, populous and well-connected state unnatural actions will inevitably be taken, and we human beings will thus be caught up in cycles of violence. To avoid this, then, we must go back to the stage of small, isolated and sparsely populated states. The crucial difference between the *Lao Zi* and the *Han Fei Zi* seems to be that Han Fei Zi believed he had found the natural laws of politics that could regulate a large and populous state, and prevent it going down the path of self-destruction. In this sense, Han Fei Zi would have seen himself as one who follows the basic teachings of the *Lao Zi* and improves upon them; that is, he would have thought of himself as a successor to the *Lao Zi*. In the following sections, in illustrating Han Fei Zi's system of political philosophy, we will register more profound agreements with the *Lao Zi*.

The reality of human beings

What natural laws of politics did Han Fei Zi discover? As we saw in Chapter 1, a crucial issue for all Chinese political philosophers during the SAWS was to find a new social glue. The glue that Han Fei Zi settled on is our natural love of fame and fortune, and the political institutions of reward and punishment – he calls them the 'two handles' (*Han Fei Zi* Chapter 7) – that are the basis of this natural love. The opening lines of Chapter 48 of the *Han Fei Zi* read:

> To govern the world the reality [*qing* 情][3] of human beings has to be followed. The reality of human beings is that they have likes and dislikes, and thus reward and punishment can be applied. If reward and punishment are applicable, prohibitions and orders can be established, and the way of governance can be completed.[4]

One can interpret this passage as conveying a neutral message. For example, one can say that we human beings like humanity and righteousness, two core Confucian values. But it is hard to imagine how one can deploy these qualities in terms of reward and punishment, for this would suggest that the likes and dislikes are concrete. A few lines later, Han Fe Zi reveals what he has in mind:

> Now, rewards should be heavy [*hou* 厚, literally 'thick'], so that the people will consider them profitable; praise should be attractive, so that the people will consider them glorious.

It becomes clear in this passage that the likes and dislikes that Han Fei Zi has in mind are profit (in the narrow sense) and fame, and not something internal. In another passage, he expresses his understanding more explicitly: 'People like profit and the position of an official [lu 祿, which means good fortune or government payment to an official, and can thus mean the position of an official], and dislike punishment' (*Han Fei Zi* Chapter 55).

What, then, of the social glue that early Confucians discovered and promoted, namely humanity or the compassion we have for strangers? Han Fei Zi does not deny that people have the capacity to show natural kindness toward strangers. He claims: 'In the fall of a year of plenty, it is considered necessary to feed even a stranger' (*Han Fei Zi* Chapter 49). Yet immediately before this claim, he maintains that 'In the spring of a year of famine, even one's little brother is not fed.' Thus, according to Han Fei Zi, our kindness is too tenuous to resist any serious challenges.

Ancients versus moderns

According to Han Fei Zi, the age of modernity is unfortunately a tough age. He states: 'In high antiquity the competition was based upon virtues, in the middle ages the contest was based upon wisdom and tact, and today the struggle is based upon strength' (*Han Fei Zi* Chapter 49). What accounts for these differences? What happened? According to Han Fei Zi,

> In antiquity men did not need to till, for the seeds of grass and the fruits of trees were sufficient to feed them; nor did women have to weave, for the skins of birds and beasts were sufficient to clothe them. Thus, without working hard, they had an abundance of supply. The people were few, and the goods were more than sufficient. Therefore the people did not struggle against each other. This is why neither heavy rewards were bestowed nor were severe punishments employed, but the people were orderly by themselves. But nowadays people do not regard five sons as many. Each son in his turn has five sons, so that before the death of the grandfather

he has twenty-five grandsons. This is why people are plenty and goods are scarce; people have to work hard and assiduously, but the supply is still rather meagre. Therefore people struggle against each other, and although rewards are doubled and punishments are applied repeatedly disorder is still inevitable. (Chapter 49)

Therefore, according to Han Fei Zi, it was natural population growth that led to relative scarcity of goods, which then led to wars and strife. The differing realities of 'ancients' and 'moderns' are the deep reason for the apparent moral decline of the masses today. He observes:

Those of antiquity made light of material goods, not because they were humane, but because material goods were abundant; those of today struggle with each other and snatch from each other, not because they are vicious, but because material goods are scarce. (Chapter 49)

Now, what of the ruling class, especially the sage-rulers who, according to Confucians, gave up their throne to someone worthy instead of to a family member? Han Fei Zi argues that in antiquity rulers such as Yao and Yu had no more than a gatekeeper, not even a slave, while in 'modernity' a county magistrate could offer a good living to generations of his descendants.

Thus, in the matter of relinquishing office, men make light of resigning from the position of the Son of Heaven [i.e. ruler of the world] in antiquity, but find it hard to give up the magistrate office of a county today; this is because of the different realities with regard to the thickness and thinness [of the benefits]. (Chapter 49)

That is,

Men made light of resigning from the position of the Son of Heaven not because they are high-minded, but because the advantage is thin [slight]; men fight for office in government or attaching themselves to those in office, not because they are lowly, but because the power [that they will acquire through this fight] is heavy [great]. (Chapter 49)

For Han Fei Zi, then, the rulers, even the Confucian sage-rulers, are no better than the masses. When the profit and fame are great, they will bow down to them, and not to humanity.

Some clarifications are needed. Han Fei Zi argues that the age of antiquity was an age of plenty, while the age of modernity is an age of scarcity. But he also argues that the rulers of antiquity were compensated meagrely, while the officials of modernity are paid handsomely. There seems to be a contradiction here, but it is easy to resolve. The plenty of antiquity is relative. Clearly, the masses back then lived poorly compared with the standard of 'modern' times (i.e. Han Fei Zi's times), eating grass seeds and fruit and wearing skins of birds and beasts. But at the time they could easily satisfy their needs. We have made progress since the time of antiquity, but our desires have increased at the same or at an even faster pace. This echoes a central message in the *Lao Zi*: that technological progress does not resolve the conflict between our limitless desires and the limited goods that can satisfy us, but only makes it worse. For what drives our desires is not satisfaction on an absolute scale, but on a relative scale. The masses today may live much better than the kings and queens of the past, but they are not happy because others have a great deal more than they do, and resources are too scarce for everyone to attain the same level as the rich and powerful.

So, why did the rulers of antiquity receive a relatively small income? Han Fei Zi does not say. We might speculate that in the days when politics was relatively simple, rulers had limited responsibilities. The population was small, meaning that there could not be a great concentration of wealth. There also existed few durable luxuries that the rulers could hoard.[5] Yet in this period of human history, as indicated in the previous chapter, it is likely that people were already involved in wars that were far more brutal than those in later periods. The period in which moral authority played a crucial role in regulating the state may have been not in antiquity, but rather, as other passages in Chapter 49 reveal, that of the Western Zhou dynasty, when the feudal system was bound together by noble codes of conduct. Han Fei Zi's analysis of antiquity as a peaceful and easy-going era may no longer be considered wholly accurate, although his view of modernity as fundamentally a harsh era still stands.

In the opening lines of Chapter 49, by means of a few historical or quasi-historical examples, Han Fei Zi shows that the sage-rulers of different ages were trying to address disparate problems, and that to attempt to apply the solution of one age to another would have been ridiculous. The true sage-ruler would adjust solutions to the age in which he lived. After offering another example in which he shows that politics based upon humanity worked in the age of antiquity but does not work in the age of modernity, he concludes that 'situations differ with the age' and that 'measures differ according to the situation' (Chapter 49). An enlightened ruler, by Han Fei Zi's standard, does not say, regardless of context, that a particular political measure is too harsh or too soft. Rather, he considers the relative abundance and scarcity of goods, and examines how great the power of a given position is (Chapter 49). In the age of modernity, rich rewards and severe punishments are necessary; the Confucians, who still appealed to the virtues, are ignoring the fact that times have changed. He says:

> Thus, antiquity and today have different customs, and new and old have different measures. Those who wish to use the government of generous and relaxed times to rule the people of chaotic times are like those wishing to stop a runaway horse without using reins and whips. This is the danger of ignorance. (Chapter 49)

The unreliability of familial care and the unresolvable conflict between private and public

However, a Confucian can argue that our kindness towards others is strong within the family. If we develop this familial care and apply it to strangers, it will be strong enough to serve as the glue to bind a big society together. But Han Fei Zi is unpersuaded by this notion, considering its efficacy unpredictable, especially when compared with measures based upon reward and punishment. Not all mothers are loving, and it takes a loving mother years to raise a son. Furthermore, even 'a loving mother may have spoiled children', whereas 'in a strict household there are no unruly slaves' (*Han Fei Zi* Chapter 50). So, for him, to rely on familial love is costly and unreliable, whereas the strict application of reward and punishment is relatively cheap and dependable. In Chapter 49, Han Fei Zi offers a more elaborate account:

> Now here is a young man of bad character. His parents rail at him, but he does not change. The respectful and honourable in the village [*xiang ren* 夕人, the village officials in charge of proper conduct and similar affairs] scold him, but he is not moved. His teachers cultivate him, but he refuses to change his ways. Thus, although the three fine influences are applied to him – the love of his parents, the conduct of the respectful and honourable in the village, and the wisdom of the teachers – he remains unmoved and not even a hair on his shins is altered. But when the local magistrates send out government soldiers to enforce the state law and search for wicked men, he becomes fearful, changes his characteristic conduct, and reforms his deeds. So the love of parents is not sufficient to educate children, and [in order for them to reform their ways] it is necessary to rely on the strict penalties of the local magistrates. This is because people are naturally spoiled by love and obedient to authority. (Chapter 49)

Moreover, according to Han Fei Zi, there is an irresolvable conflict between familial love (private) and state interest (public). He offers two stories to illustrate this point. Clearly with Confucians as the target, one story is his own version of the mutual concealment case (cf. *Analects* 13.18, which was discussed in Chapter 2); the other story has Confucius as a main character. In the first story, an upright person of the state of Chu turns in his sheep-stealing father, but the prime minister orders the son to be executed because his deed, though showing loyalty to the king, was unfilial to his father. To Han Fei Zi, this shows that 'the upright subject of a king is a brutal son of the father' (Chapter 49). In the other story, someone from the state of Lu has deserted from three battles. When Confucius asks him why, he answers that in the event of his death there would be no one to take care of his old father. Judging him filial, Confucius recommends him for promotion. To Han Fei Zi, this shows that 'a filial son of a father is a disobedient subject of the king' (Chapter 49). He then sums up the lesson of these stories:

> Then, following the execution of the upright man by the prime minister, no other bad people and deeds in Chu were ever reported to the authorities; following the rewarding [of the deserter] by Confucius, the people of Lu were apt to surrender or run away. The interests of superior and inferior are as different as all these, and so it is hopeless for the ruler to commend the deeds of the common man and at the same time to try to ensure the blessing to the state's altars of the soil and grain. (Chapter 49)

Then, tracing the etymology of the terms for 'private' and 'public', he shows that, from the very invention of these characters, the conflict between the private and the public was already known.[6]

Truly virtuous people are useless at governing

But clearly there were high-minded Confucians who cultivated their familial care and devoted themselves to the interests of the people and the state. According to Han Fei Zi, however, such people are too few in number and thus cannot be relied upon to maintain the order of the state. In contrast, when political institutions are based on the principle of reward and punishment, everyone can be made useful in the cause of supporting the state's interest. He argues that 'the people will bow naturally to authority, but few of them can be moved by righteousness'. There was only one person in the world, Confucius, who truly practised humanity and righteousness. This sage 'cultivated his conduct, exemplified the Way, and travelled' across the world. And he had only seventy avowed followers, all of whom loved humanity and righteousness. This, according to Han Fei Zi, shows how rare and difficult it is to cherish humanity and practise virtuousness. In contrast, when Duke Ai of Lu, an inferior ruler, was the sovereign of the state, no one, not even Confucius, dared not to acknowledge allegiance to him, not because Duke Ai was humane but because he held the position of the sovereign. Han Fei Zi concludes:

> Now, when scholars counsel a ruler, they do not urge him to wield authority, which is the certain way to success, but insist that he must practise humanity and righteousness, which will make him a [true] king. This is to require every ruler to rise to the level of Confucius, and all the ordinary people of the time to be like Confucius's disciples. Such a measure is bound to fail! (Chapter 49)

Indeed, for Han Fei Zi, not only can the ruler not rely on virtuous people because they are few in number, but he does not really need them. Discussing a special kind of virtuous person, one who is trustworthy and does not cheat, he again points out that such individuals are too few to fill all the governmental offices. Moreover, he explains why such people are valued by the masses, and why a ruler does not need to value them. He argues that those who value virtuous individuals who do not cheat do so because they have no means to protect themselves from being exploited other than by finding people who do not cheat. That is, 'The commoners in selecting friends have neither wealth to benefit others nor power and authority to intimidate others, and thus they seek for gentlemen who do not cheat [to be friends with].' In contrast,

> the ruler occupies a position whereby he can control others, and he possesses the wealth of a state. He may dispense great rewards and severe punishments. If he uses them wisely, even the most deceitful subjects would not dare to cheat him. Thus, the ruler does not need those with a trustworthy character. (Chapter 49)

Therefore 'those who govern [should] employ [what is effective for] the many, and discard [what is effective for] the few. Hence they devote themselves not to virtues, but to laws and regulations' (Chapter 50). Then, in his characteristically beautiful rhetoric that often employs powerful analogies, he says that it is hopeless to wait for an arrow's shaft to become straight by itself, or for a piece of wood to become round by itself. Even if this were possible, they could not be so valued because there would be so few of them, whereas there is a great need for arrows and wheels. The reality is that arrows and chariots are produced and used because there exist tools for straightening and bending.

The teachings of the wise are applicable neither to the many nor to the few

According to his rationale that what is needed in governance is what is applicable to the many and not merely to the few, Han Fei Zi also criticizes the use of the teachings of the wise. In line with his low expectation of the strength of virtue among human beings, Han Fei Zi believes that the masses lack wisdom. They are like babies who cry over the painful cures for their ailments because they '[do] not understand that the small amount of pain they suffer will bring great benefit to them' (Chapter 50). He cites historical examples in which the masses slandered and threw rocks at the great rulers who tried to help them (Chapter 50). What is commonly considered wisdom is, for Han Fei Zi, 'subtle and mysterious words'. These words

> even the wisest men have difficulty understanding. Now if you try to set up laws for the masses on the basis of what the wisest men have difficulty understanding, then there is no way for the masses to learn them. Those who do not get their fill of the coarsest grain do not seek fine millet and meat, and those who do not have rags do not expect to have embroidered robes. In dealing with governmental affairs, when you haven't solved the urgent matters you should not address what is not urgent. Now in terms of political measures for governing and dealing with the people, if you do not use what any man and woman can plainly understand, but long to apply the doctrines of the wisest men, then that is the opposite of good governance. Subtle and mysterious words are no business of the people. (Chapter 49)

Together with his criticism of rulers' valuing trustworthiness, Han Fei Zi concludes: 'Thus the Way of an enlightened ruler is to stick to laws instead of seeking for the wise, and to retain measures [of reward and punishment] instead of longing for the trustworthy' (Chapter 49).

There is a further problem with the teachings of the wise: they are destined to be pluralistic. Han Fei Zi is arguably the first thinker to argue that a pluralism of thought is inevitable in the history of ideas. He believes that even if we follow the teachings of the wise or the comprehensive doctrine of one school, teachings should be a unity, so that we can know exactly what to do in this or that particular situation. Unfortunately such unity is wanting. He writes:

> The eminent learnings in the present age are Confucianism and Mohism. The highest figure of Confucianism is Confucius, and the highest figure of Mohism is Mo Zi. . . . Since Confucius and Mo Zi, the Confucian school has split into eight factions, and the Mohist school into three. What they adopt and discard are contradictory to and different from each other, and yet each claims itself to be true to the teachings of Confucius and Mo Zi. Confucius and Mo Zi cannot come back to life, so who is to decide which doctrine in the present age is the right one? (Chapter 50)

Similarly, both Confucianism and Mohism claim to be true to the teachings of Yao and Shun the sage-rulers. Yao and Shun cannot come back to life to decide which of the two mutually contradictory doctrines is correct; moreover, a very long time has passed since the age of Yao and Shun, and so it is simply impossible to figure out what constitutes their genuine teachings. We might add that Han Fei Zi observes that even the wisest men find subtle and mysterious teachings hard to decipher, which suggests that even they could not agree on how to interpret them. Thus pluralism of thought is inevitable (unless oppression is practised), and no comprehensive moral doctrine will produce agreement, even among the few.

Han Fei Zi, Xun Zi and modern European thought

Two points of clarification are in order before we discuss the next topic. First, Han Fei Zi is said to have been a pupil of Xun Zi. Some passages in the *Han Fei Zi* are similar and sometimes even identical to passages in the *Xun Zi*. Han Fei Zi's low expectation of human beings will also remind the reader of Xun Zi's claim that human beings are by nature bad. Yet we perceive a crucial difference between Han Fei Zi and Xun Zi in their evaluations of human nature. Although Xun Zi, unlike Mencius, does not believe we have an inborn and natural tendency to be good, they agree that human beings should and can be good in a Confucian sense. Since Xun Zi recognizes our lack of innate goodness, it is more important for him than for Mencius that we should work hard to improve ourselves. As we have seen, Han Fei Zi acknowledged that we can be kind to others, when there is no economic pressure, but he refuted the notion that we can ever reliably improve our moral character. For him, this is a fact of life that is a building block of our political structure, and we should not mistakenly try to change it. Thus, even though Han Fei Zi was a pupil of Xun Zi, he clearly did not agree with his teacher on human nature. He was not the only one to have betrayed his teacher, of course; indeed, oftentimes the greatness of a pupil lies in his ability to betray the teachings of his master.

Second, Han Fei Zi's teachings are often compared with those of Niccolò Machiavelli, Thomas Hobbes and some other Western thinkers, although there exists no close study of their similarities and differences. For example, in the opening statement of *An Introduction to the Principles of Morals and Legislation*, the English utilitarian philosopher Jeremy Bentham plainly states that pain and pleasure are the sole and supreme masters of human beings (1949: 1). He then goes on to demonstrate that religious and moral values, if taken as the basis of government and legislation, will lead to either despotism (when we impose one set of values on all) or anarchy (when anything goes), and to show how these values are merely utility misapplied

(Bentham 1949: 1–23; chs 1 and 2). Yet there are subtle and important differences between Han Fei Zi and Bentham. For example, Han Fei Zi never claimed that moral values are illusory; rather, people have the capacity to be truly moral when goods are abundant (relative to human desires), or in a small group of people. Reward and punishment and the political institutions based upon them become important when there is a need to create a bond between the members of a large society. In other words, Han Fei Zi saw that the debate over antiquity versus modernity connects to the question regarding few and many: what works when the state is small and people are few (antiquity) does not work in a large and populous state (modernity). Thus, not only did Han Fei Zi's thought reflect the shift from antiquity to modernity, but he was conscious of the nature of this change. In contrast, Bentham did not seem to be keenly aware of the transformation. Similarly, if we wish to compare Han Fei Zi with Machiavelli, Hobbes and others, to assert a similarity on the simple basis of their shared denial of the significance of the virtues is hardly adequate. Rather, it is important that we investigate whether and how they deny the significance of the virtues, which it is that they discount, and what the reasons are for their denial.

The strength of a state and the five vermin

We have seen that, according to Han Fei Zi, the use of reward and punishment and the political institutions (laws, regulations, bureaucracy, etc.) built upon them enable people to be manipulated into doing whatever the ruler wants them to do. What, then, should the ruler want them to do? What is the goal of the ruler? It is to make the state strong. For Han Fei Zi, a state's strength is measured according to how many crops it harvests and how many enemy heads its people chop off. A state, then, should promote farming and military achievement, and nothing else. What the Confucian literati and the Mohists promote is detrimental to this goal. They are thus designated the two most eminent 'vermin' of the five enemies of the state – 'Five Vermin' being the title of Chapter 49 of the *Han Fei Zi*. Confucians promoted (Confucian) virtues and traditions, and Mohists are often associated with the 'private swordsman' (*si jian* 私剑) or *xia* 侠. The latter term lacks an easy translation. Xia were Robin Hood-like private swordsmen who tried to maintain justice on their own by killing 'bad guys' or killing out of loyalty to those to whom they pledged allegiance. For want of a better translation, we'll call them 'wandering knights', though we must bear in mind that they lacked (or had already lost – in the transition from feudalism to modernity) the official status enjoyed by the European knights, and they were not necessarily horsemen. According to Han Fei Zi, 'Confucian literati disturb laws with their letters, and wandering knights violate prohibitions with their martial art' (Chapter 49). We can readily understand the latter, as we know what activities these wandering knights engaged in, which included avenging killings outside the authority of the state. As for the former, Han Fei Zi's point becomes clear if we recall what Mencius said about the justified removal of a tyrannical king. Although it may seem a good proposition to remove a despotic ruler, for Han Fei Zi it can never be crystal clear when a ruler is really bad, given the inevitable plurality of sophisticated doctrines in the modern age. For him, Mencius's claim can only end up by creating confusion and giving an excuse to would-be usurpers.

For Han Fei Zi, then, the state must have order and thus needs authority-respecting and law-abiding people. Confucians and Mohists, on the other hand, are perceived as a challenge to this very order. Moreover, he observes that 'to enrich a state depends upon farmers, and to resist enemies depends upon soldiers' (Chapter 49). The literati do not produce crops, and the wandering knights are not that useful in wars, especially in the people's wars that emerged during the SAWS. Thus, they have no utility for the state. Unfortunately, given that these two schools are dominant, confused rulers often value them. This undermines the morale of those the state truly needs: farmers and soldiers. By means of many arguments and stories, Han Fei Zi writes extensively on this point in Chapter 49. According to him, to farm and to fight in war are tough and demanding. People perform these tasks only if there exists a regime of reward and punishment. If they see that they can have the reward without doing the hard work – that is, if they can get it by studying books and becoming learned, like the literati – they will eschew farming and soldiering without a second thought. Private individuals will naturally have a positive view of this state of affairs, but the state should not share this. Again, an enlightened ruler should understand the conflict between private and public interests. Han Fei Zi even attacked those who were learned in the Legalist tradition and in military strategy. He opines:

> Now the people within the boundary [of the state] all talk about good government, and every family has a copy of the works on political measures by Shang Yang and Guan Zhong 管仲.[7] But the state is becoming poorer and poorer. This is because many talk about tillage but few take up the plough. Everybody within the boundary [of the state] talks about military affairs, and every family has a copy of the works of Sun Zi and Wu Qi [who wrote on military strategies]. But the army is becoming weaker and weaker. This is because many talk about warfare but few put on armour. Therefore the enlightened ruler makes use of men's strength but does not listen to their words; he rewards their achievements but prohibits useless activities. (Chapter 49)

Thus Han Fei Zi wishes to see clear results, and is inclined to base rewards and punishments on them. All empty talk will be ignored. He concludes:

> Therefore, in the state of an enlightened ruler, there are no letters written on bamboo slips, and laws supply the instruction. There are no sermons of the early kings, and the magistrates serve as the instructors. There are no fierce feuds of private swordsmen, and chopping off the heads [of the enemy] is considered the deed of valor. (Chapter 49)

On the basis of similar considerations, Han Fei Zi views commerce and artisanship as vermin in the state as well. For, according to him, they do not really increase the strength of the state. Like the literati and the private swordsmen, the men of commerce and artisans only waste the grain of the state. Worse still, shrewd businessmen make easy money, and will thus damage the morale of the farmers. They can also use bribery to advance their position and avoid fighting in wars. They, too, should be restricted to the merely necessary, if not totally eliminated.

Traditional Chinese culture is said to have disparaged commerce. Can this claim be sustained, and if so which school or schools were responsible for the development of such an outlook? We find no clear evidence in early Confucian writings. They were only against wealth that was not accumulated in a rightful manner. Confucius advises in the *Analects*:

> When the Way prevails in the state and you are poor and in a lowly position, be ashamed of yourself; when the Way does not prevail in the state and you are wealthy and in an honourable position, be ashamed of yourself. (8.13)

And we have seen in *Mencius* (3A4) that Mencius considers it unjust to sell things of different quality at the same price. Of the three prominent Chinese schools of political thought, it is the Daoist (the *Lao Zi*) and the Legalist (*Han Fei Zi*), and not the Confucian, that tend to disparage commerce.

From a contemporary point of view, we might find Han Fei Zi's economic outlook strange. Yet it is interesting to note that the French Physiocrats in the eighteenth century had views that were apparently similar. This will be touched on again in later discussion.

Also considered a verminous presence on the state is the lobbyist/ diplomat, who tries to forge alliances among states. Han Fei Zi does not think highly of such diplomacy. Those who pursued this activity, according to him, were out for their own self-interest, committed to making a profit regardless of the consequences to the states involved. To depend on protection from another state or to protect other states through alliances can only sap the strength of the states involved. In the former case, there is no guarantee that protection will actually be forthcoming, but it is guaranteed that the stronger state from which a state seeks protection will take advantage of the weaker state. In the latter case, there is no guarantee that saving a weaker state will be advantageous to the stronger state (for the weaker state may not feel gratitude in the future when under new pressures), and it is almost guaranteed that the strength of the strong state that tries to defend the weaker will be eroded. Generally speaking, contrary to the claim of the lobbyist/diplomat that 'to attend to foreign affairs can at best make one a king, and at least can offer security [to his state]' (Chapter 49), Han Fei Zi thought that 'making a state secure and strong cannot rely upon things external, but is dependent upon internal governance' (Chapter 49).

Probably with his home state in mind, which was perhaps the weakest of the seven strong states in the Warring States period, Han Fei Zi argues that diplomacy is a dangerous tool for a weak state to use in order to survive. A strong state can try different tactics, and can afford to fail on occasion. It may thus appear to be good at strategy and diplomacy. As the proverb says, 'Those who possess a great deal of money are skilful in trading' (Chapter 49). This implies that if you have little money, one wrong move can sink your entire business. Thus, instead of appealing to diplomacy, weak states should

> hurry to improve the political order within their boundaries, make clear their laws and prohibitions, make certain their rewards and punishments, utilize their natural resources to increase provisions, and lead their people to strengthen the defence of their cities to the point of death. Then the world would find little gain in occupying their land and great harm in attacking their states, so that even a state of ten thousand chariots would not dare to be trapped next to their fortified city walls and expose its weaknesses to the attack of [other] strong enemies. This is the way to escape destruction. (Chapter 49)

In spite of Han Fei Zi's disparagement of scheming in diplomacy, his own theory of war is rather shrewd. It compares with the manner in which Socrates discusses the defence of a small yet strongly unified city-state (*Republic* 422a–423c). Yet Socrates does appeal to diplomacy, to take advantage of factions within and among other states. Notably, compared to what Mencius says about the defence of a small state (*Mencius* 1B13–15), discussed in Chapter 2, both Han Fei Zi's and Socrates' accounts lack consideration for humanity and show no compassion towards the people of other states.

The last category of vermin in the state is those who evade military duty by pledging allegiance to a powerful lord. This reduces the pool of soldiers, and boosts the power of certain factions within the state. The harm done by this kind of person is obvious.

Complementing Han Fei Zi's stance on the strength of the state and what is detrimental to it is an opposition to certain aspects of welfare assistance. He argues that, other conditions (such as health, good or bad harvest, fortune, being free or imprisoned, or outside income) being equal, the well-to-do must be hard-working and frugal; the poor and destitute must be lazy and spendthrift. Thus, against the view of scholars of his time that good government should 'give land to the poor and destitute so that those who have no means of livelihood may be provided for', Han Fei Zi argues that the political agenda implied by this idea is to take from the hard-working and the frugal and give to the spendthrift and lazy, which is bad for the state (Chapter 50). His argument anticipates, for example, the contemporary challenge to (heavy) taxation and the welfare state on the part of American conservatives.

A bureaucracy chosen on the basis of results

To sum up, according to Han Fei Zi, the most effective tool of governance is the political application of reward and punishment. The goal of the state is to make itself strong; strength lies in farming and military prowess. The five vermin should be clamped down on and even eliminated; hard-working farmers and brave soldiers, both of whom are law-fearing subjects, should be encouraged. The next issue is how to select and evaluate members of the bureaucracy. As we saw from Shang Yang's reform, in common with the Confucians the Legalists did not wish to go back to feudalism; they wanted to establish a meritocracy. But for them, Confucian virtues and wisdom do not constitute merits; they value only the growth of crops and the chopping off of heads. After showing how even the wise Confucius made mistakes when he judged people's merits on the basis of their appearances or their rhetoric, Han Fei Zi argues:

> Simply by observing someone's appearance and dress, and listening to his speech, even Confucius cannot be certain about what kind of gentlemen he is. But if you try him out in a government office, and examine his achievements, then even the mediocre man will be in no doubt as to his slow-wittedness or intelligence. Therefore, among the magistrates under an enlightened ruler, the prime minister must have arisen from the post of the district magistrate, and the gallant generals must have emerged from low ranks. If it is certain that a person with achievements is rewarded, then he rises in title and salary, and he is given more and more encouragement [to do better]. (Chapter 50)

This passage clearly shows how Han Fei Zi envisioned an ideal meritocratic bureaucracy based upon farming and military achievement, and driven purely by results.

Elsewhere, Han Fei Zi offers a more detailed account of the examination of an individual's merits, by means of comparing words with deeds. Here is the process:

> The official comes forward to present his proposal; the ruler assigns him a task on the basis of this proposal, and concentrates on demanding the accomplishment of the task. If the achievement fits the task, and the task fits the proposal, the official is rewarded. If the achievement does not fit the task, and the task does not fit the proposal, the official is punished. (Chapter 7)

Obviously if one fails to achieve the task in hand, punishment is justified. This is quite intuitive. But Han Fei Zi also claims that overachievement should be punished as well. He tells a story a few lines after the account quoted above. A Marquis got drunk and fell asleep. The keeper of the royal hat laid a robe on him to protect him from the cold. When the Marquis discovered this, he punished both this keeper and the keeper of the royal robe. Punishing the robe keeper is easily understandable: he failed to do his job. But why was the hat keeper also punished? The formal reason is that he carried out an unauthorized task. But why is this perceived to be dangerous? In the previous chapter, Han Fei Zi cautions:

> The process by which ministers invade [the rights of] their sovereign is like the way the contour of the landscape [misleads a walker]: the topography changes gradually and his orientation alters from facing east to facing west. But he is not aware of it [because of the gradual change]. (Chapter 6)

Thus, an official who overachieves or who takes on the task of another, although apparently of good intention, will mislead the ruler. He may have done it intentionally in order to usurp eventually the power of the ruler. Or he may have done it with no ill intention. But it may subsequently become a habit and thus disturb the order of the state. Indeed, Han Fei Zi envisions his bureaucracy as a well-functioning and efficient machine, and this requires every part to do whatever job it is supposed to do. If a part overachieves its task or takes on another part's task, this might seem to be good, but from the point of view of the whole it is very bad and should be remedied.

The ideal ruler, governing with no (human) action

We discussed the puzzling issue of Han Fei Zi's appreciation of the *Lao Zi*, and offered the explanation that, when the political structure of the state is built on the basis of the Way, everything is done according to the natural laws of politics and is thus effected without the need for human action. As we have seen, this is the case with ministers: they take no initiative, and do only what their position requires them to do. Such a minister 'follows the lead of his ruler and obeys the laws of the sovereign. He empties his mind to await orders and does not question whether they are right or wrong' (Chapter 6).

To ensure that ministers engage in no unnatural deeds, the orders from the ruler have to be natural – that is, based upon the natural laws of politics. This means that the ruler has to follow the natural Way and must empty his own mind as well. This is precisely what Han Fei Zi suggests in the opening lines of the chapter entitled 'The Way of the Ruler':

> The Way is the beginning of all things and the measure [ji 纪] of right and wrong. Therefore the enlightened ruler holds to the beginning in order to know the origin of all things, and minds the measure in order to know the cause of good and bad, success and failure. Therefore, empty and still, he awaits orders [from the Way], letting names define themselves and affairs settle by themselves. (Chapter 5)

Chapter 49 ('Five Vermin') and Chapter 50 ('Eminent Learning') are the chapters on which readers of the Han Fei Zi tend to focus, for they present incisive attacks on Confucianism, which is often taken as the dominant school of Chinese thought. But if we wish to understand Han Fei Zi's conception of the ideal regime, Chapters 5–8 might be a better starting point. The problem arises, though, that the somewhat abstract, theoretical and even mystical expressions employed in these chapters are difficult to understand. However, now that we have an understanding of his view of human nature, the political institutions built upon it, what benefits the state, and a system of meritocratic appointment informed by verifiable results – all of which conform to the natural laws of politics (as construed) – we are in a better position to understand his theoretical model.

In the opening lines of Chapter 5, quoted above, what Han Fei Zi seems to be suggesting is that the ruler should not determine policy on the basis of his own (human) wisdom and understanding of virtue, but follow what the laws of nature dictate. Elsewhere, he makes this point more explicitly.

The enlightened ruler uses laws[8] to select people, and does not recommend someone by himself; he uses laws to measure achievements, and does not deliberate by himself. (Chapter 6)

Why should the ruler not rely on his own wisdom and virtues? One reason may be that Han Fei Zi shared with the *Lao Zi* the view that humans were deficient when measured against the natural Way. That is, the natural Way is so powerful and we human beings are so inadequate in comparison that taking matters into our own hands will only backfire. The philosophy of the *Lao Zi* is often likened to the notion of laissez-faire in governance and economy. The latter is said to originate, in the West, with the Physiocrats. Earlier we saw that Han Fei Zi's emphasis on the significance of agriculture to the strength of the state was echoed in the thinking of the Physiocrats, and here we register another resonance between them. Indeed, in spite of Han Fei Zi's and the *Lao Zi*'s abhorrence of commerce, there is a fundamental similarity between their philosophy and modern economic theory: both are suspicious of human (a term Han Fei Zi and the *Lao Zi* favour) or central (the term preferred by modern economic theory) planning. Both consider it hubris to maintain that we can plan our way forward humanly, and believe that we have no option but to rely on the invisible hand of natural laws (of politics for Han Fei Zi and of economics for modern economic theorists).[9]

Other reasons are suggested by Han Fei Zi for asking rulers not to undertake 'unnatural' actions. For one thing, the state is by now much too large and the bureaucracy far too complicated for a ruler with a busybody style to manage. He says:

If the ruler has to monitor all officials himself, he will find the day not long enough and his energy insufficient. Moreover, if the superior person uses his eyes, the inferior will ornament their appearances; if the superior person uses his ears, the inferior will ornament what they say; and if the superior person deliberates, the inferior will offer sophisticated rhetoric. Regarding these three [faculties] as insufficient, the early kings left aside their own abilities, relied on laws and policies, and acted carefully with reward and punishment. Since the early kings held fast to what was fundamental, their laws were simple and not violated.

Then, although the ideal ruler 'ruled over all within the four seas by himself', no cunning and callous people dared to employ their tricks, and officials near and far dared not disobey orders or cover up any deeds. They all do the jobs that they are supposed to do.

> Thus affairs of government are not enough [to occupy the ruler completely] and there is free time [for the ruler to spend]. The way in which the ruler relies upon his position makes it so.[10]

Governing with uniform and strict laws

We can see that, in order to have a non-active yet effective government in the large and populous modern state, the universal application of law is necessary, and certain conditions facilitate such an application. From Han Fei Zi's attack on virtues, discussed earlier, we learned that, for him, virtues cannot serve as an effective glue to bind the state together, but laws can. To achieve this degree of effectiveness, laws have to be simple enough for the masses to understand and for ministers and the ruler to administrate with. Simplicity also prevents laws from being twisted and discreetly violated. Laws must have authority for people to follow them. This requires that they be feared, and strictly and consistently followed. For the authority of laws to be upheld, and to prevent the ruler and the magistrates from becoming meddlers, laws must be impartial and blind.

We quoted earlier a passage from Chapter 49 in which Han Fei Zi argues that a bad son cannot be corrected by familial love, moral exemplar and instruction, but is readily disciplined with strict laws. He then offers some analogies. For example, a great climber would be unable to scale a modest city wall, but a crippled sheep could climb up a high mountain. This is because the former is steep, while the latter is not. 'Therefore the enlightened ruler makes his laws steep and his punishments severe.' Ordinary people are unwilling to give up a few feet of cloth, but even a good thief would not take a large amount of molten gold. That is because it is certain that to do the latter would harms one's hands.

> Therefore the enlightened ruler makes his punishments definite. For this reason rewards should not be other than great and trustable, making people consider them profitable; punishments should not be other than heavy and definite, making people fear them; and laws should not be other than uniform and inflexible, making people understand them. Consequently, if the ruler in bestowing rewards makes no change and in carrying out punishments grants no pardon, and lets praise accompany rewards and disparagement attend punishments, then both the worthy and the unworthy will exert their best efforts. (Chapter 49)

Elsewhere, after arguing for the necessity of making rewards desirable and punishments severe, Han Fei Zi says:

> Thus the enlightened ruler is never overliberal in his rewards, and is never overlenient in his punishments. If his rewards are too liberal, even the ministers of merit will be lax in their duties; if his punishments are too lenient, villainous ministers will be liable to do wrong. Therefore, if a man has truly achieved a desirable result, no matter how distant [from the ruler's inner circle or bloodline] and humble he may be, he must be rewarded; if a man has truly made a mistake, no matter how close and dear [to the ruler] he may be, he must be punished.

Doing so will make the distant and humble diligent and prevent the close and dear becoming arrogant (Chapter 5). With the authority of the law established, and with laws uniformly and strictly followed, there is at least procedural justice in the state, which is a necessary step to the rule of law and constitutionalism, inventions that are often attributed to Western modernity.

Do not govern on the basis of personal preferences or human criteria

If the ruler fails to remain 'still' (detached and non-active) and 'empty' (dispassionate and refraining from using one's own wisdom), and tries to use his own preferences to resolve political matters, his subjects will cease to be non-active, the consequence of which could be dangerous to the power and authority of the ruler. These qualities in a ruler are the necessary condition for his subjects, especially his ministers, to behave likewise. As a passage in Chapter 6 details, when the ruler uses his own faculties and applies his own preferences, his ministers will adopt a pretence that appeals to the ruler. But if the ruler does not do so, the ministers will reveal their true selves. This will prevent them engaging in treacherous activities, and will give the ruler a good idea of who they are and what is the best task for them. Han Fei Zi says:

> The ruler does not reveal his desires. If he reveals his desires, the ministers will polish their manners accordingly. The ruler does not reveal his will. If he reveals his will, the ministers will display a different appearance. So it is said, discard likes and dislikes and the ministers will reveal their inornate selves. Discard wisdom and wile and the ministers will watch their step.

By undertaking no unnatural actions, by not being wise or brave (i.e. not applying their own wisdom and courage), the ministers will precisely be wise and brave, fulfilling their duties as prescribed by laws and institutions, and will be judged on the basis of their concrete achievements (Chapter 5). Han Fei Zi's play on the apparently counter-intuitive ideas that not putting to use (the ruler's) wisdom can lead to the exercise of wisdom (by the ministers), and (the ruler's) being not brave can lead to bravery (on the part of the generals) and strengthen the state will remind the reader of a similar play in the *Lao Zi*, although arguably Han Fei Zi gives these ideas a new interpretive twist.

One might object to the notion of non-action by arguing that if the ruler does not apply his own ideas, but instead relies on institutions and laws, the ministers and subjects will put up a facade in accordance with what the laws and institutions dictate. Thus, the hidden reasoning in Han Fei Zi's arguments for non-action is that such facades are not bad for the state. In contrast, so long as laws and orders are obeyed, the good of the state is served, even if obedience is involuntary and enforced. This is consistent with his overarching idea that what is verifiable is results, and nothing else matters. This is why he has no time for Confucian virtues based on inner worth.

In Chapter 7, Han Fei Zi offers some historical examples to demonstrate the danger of encouraging any appearance other than obedience to laws and institutions. For instance, when the personal preferences of a ruler are revealed, many people will strive to cater to them. So, when a king preferred slim waists, many people in his state chose to starve themselves. But once these people had assumed power, they committed treacherous deeds at the first opportunity. For 'the reality of ministers is that they do not necessarily love their ruler; [they cater to the ruler's desires] because they hope for great profit' (Chapter 7).

Moreover, the use of means other than performance-based criteria to select officials is also detrimental to the authority of laws, institutions, the state and, eventually, the ruler. Han Fei Zi says:

> Now, if the judgement as to whether a man is able is based upon his reputation, then the ministers will disregard the ruler and seek the praise of subordinates and peers. If appointment to office is based upon cliques, then the people will work to establish connections, and won't seek appointment in accordance with [the requirements of] laws and institutions.

As a result,

> The officials will turn their backs on law, seeking only to establish their private influences and making light of public affairs. They will flock to the gates of powerful men many times, but not even once will they come to the court of the ruler. (Chapter 6)

Elswhere, Han Fei Zi offers a similar argument. In the chapter entitled 'Eight Villainies', the fifth villainy is said to be '[buying the support of] the masses.' That is,

A minister distributes public funds to please the masses and bestows small favours to win over the people, so that both the people in the ruler's court and the people in the marketplace will praise him, in order to get what he desires by blocking the ruler['s judgements]. (Chapter 9)

Let us be clear, Han Fei Zi wished to establish a meritocracy or rule by the 'worthy' (xian 賢). His regular criticisms regarding preferment of the worthy are concerned with promotions of the wrong kind: that is, of a 'worthy' as the masses and other thinkers (for example, the Confucians) understand the term. He also maintains that praise and disparagement, indeed reputation in general, constitute an important aspect of reward and punishment – the 'two handles' of statecraft; he is only against the 'wrong' or undeserved kind of praise and disparagement. Whether or not someone is worthy should be determined by verifiable results within the legal and institutional framework. If someone is proved worthy in this way, then, as cited earlier, 'Let praise accompany rewards and let disparagement accompany punishments; then both the worthy and the unworthy will exert their best efforts' (Chapter 49).

Although Han Fei Zi was criticizing the manner of selecting officials in his day, the problems he reveals resemble in some ways those prevalent in today's democracies. Although in theory power in today's democracies lies not with one man but with the people, Han Fei Zi's argument regarding the selection of officials (or legislators) by reputation or on the basis of people's praise still holds. Legislators in today's democracies distribute public funds to their constituencies or their people to serve their particular interests (as opposed to the interests of all in the state), so as to get their support at the price of the public interest. Lobbyists and junior politicians flock to more powerful officials, catering to their interests rather than those of the people. The founders of today's democracies may have hoped that the private interests of politicians would balance each other out and become identical with the public interest, but the reality often fails to live up to this hope, thereby giving credence to Han Fei Zi's argument.

The ideal ruler: embodying the Way and being selfless

To sum up, as long as the ruler does not undertake 'unnatural' actions, but uses institutions and laws to regulate the state, his officials will behave 'naturally' as well. If the officials do not behave 'naturally', the ruler will let the institutions and the laws punish them. By not putting to use his own wisdom, moral sentiment or personal preferences, the ruler becomes identical with and the embodiment of the Way, the natural laws of politics. Thus he becomes the guarantor of the Way, making sure all under him will do as the Way dictates. This is perhaps what Han Fei Zi wishes to say in this rather abstract and Lao Zi-like passage:

> The Way is not the same as myriad things; … a scale is not the same as heaviness and lightness; … a ruler is not the same as his ministers… (Chapter 8)

Like the scale, the ruler measures the merit of his ministers, but, being the standard of measurement, the ruler himself is beyond any measurement within the system.

As indicated, some argue that gong 公, which means 'the public' in modern Chinese, should not be translated as 'the public' or 'the state', as it refers to the interests of the ruler. But, as we have seen, the ideal ruler for Han Fei Zi dispenses with his own wisdom, moral sentiment and personal preferences. In the 'Eight Villainies' (Chapter 9) as in many other places in the Han Fei Zi, Han Fei Zi argues that the ideal ruler will not try to satisfy his desires at will, but follows set rules. For example,

> Things that delight and amuse the ruler must be brought to the ruler according to set edicts, and must not be brought to him or taken away arbitrarily, thus not allowing his ministers to please him [with these things]. (Chapter 9)

Therefore, rather than being a tyrant with absolute control at will over the state – which some argue is the type of ruler Han Fei Zi had in mind – the ideal ruler is faceless and identifies himself with the state.[11] He is like a mechanical part that functions as the central control over other mechanical parts (his subjects), and all these parts together become a well-functioning machine, a state that follows the natural laws of politics.

Thus, in Han Fei Zi's ideal state, it seems that no one's interest is served, only that of the state. But why is it desirable to satisfy the interest of the state in which no one individual's interest is served?[12] Han Fei Zi anticipated people's failure to see the merit of his ideal state, believing that they would consider it tyrannical. He says:

> The sage is the one who scrutinizes the facts of right and wrong and investigates the reality of order and chaos. Therefore, when governing the state, he rectifies clear laws and establishes severe penalties, in order to save all living beings from chaos, to rid the world of misfortune, to make the strong not exploit the weak and the many not tyrannize the few, to enable the old and the infirm to die in peace and the young and the orphans to be raised, and to see to it that the frontiers not be invaded, that ruler and minister be intimate with each other, that father and son protect each other, and that there be no worry about being killed in war or taken prisoner. Such is one of the greatest achievements. Yet ignorant men do not understand it and condemn it as tyranny. (Chapter 14)

Yet there is a difference between achieving this result, which is desired by all, as a side effect and as a goal. Han Fei Zi's system doesn't seem to leave space for taking up people's interests as a concern. Moreover, even if we accept his claim that in a strong state everyone is satisfied, how can we guarantee that someone doesn't want more? In particular, the ruler has all the power: so why doesn't he use it for his own amusement or his own ends? Who can stop him from doing so? This is the question to which we now turn.

Correct the non-ideal ruler and maintain his supreme authority: a conflict?

The ideal ruler, being the embodiment of the Way within the state, sees to it that any of his subjects who dares to engage in unnatural actions is punished. But what about the non-ideal ruler? In Han Fei Zi's political design, the relations between the ruler and ministers of state and those between the Way and the ruler have a certain symmetry. That is, the Way itself sees to it that the ruler who dares to take unnatural actions is punished with the weakening or even the destruction of the state. For

> No state is forever strong or forever weak. If those who uphold laws are strong [i.e. resolute in their upholding of laws], the state is strong. If those who uphold laws are weak [i.e. irresolute], the state is weak. (Chapter 6)

We can say that on one issue key to China's early modernity, the legitimacy of the sovereign, Han Fei Zi's answer (though for him the theoretical issue may have taken second place to strengthening his home state and eventually unifying China) is a 'naturalistic' one: that is, whoever is able to maintain his power as the ruler domestically and sustain an invincible state internationally has the right to be sovereign. He can achieve this feat because he follows the natural way of politics. In this sense, then, the sovereign's legitimacy comes from nature.

As the passage quoted above shows, correction of the ruler's behaviour comes from outside. There is no internal mechanism whereby it can be rectified, just as there is no means for an enlightened ruler to correct the Way; he can only be its faithful follower. Han Fei Zi had good reason to rule out the possibility of any internal mechanism. For, being the guarantor of the Way within the state, the ruler must have authority. If it is apparent that he can be challenged, then his authority will be challenged too. Even in modern democratic states, certain institutions (such as the constitution) are held sacred. But modern democracies find a way to get around Han Fei Zi's worries. They formally separate the state and the authoritative institutions from the individuals who run them. Also there are procedures whereby even the most sacred institution can be changed without damage to its authority; an example being amendments to the American Constitution. We note the employment of a similar procedure by early Confucians. As we saw in Chapter 3, when Mencius is asked for justification for the killing of a king who turns out to be a tyrant, he is very careful to make the distinction between killing a person who happens to have the title of king but doesn't do the job this title prescribes, and regicide, the killing of one who has the title of king and does carry out his duties properly (*Mencius* 1B8).

Relating to this issue, as we saw, Han Fei Zi argues that a pluralism of values is inescapable. But rather than arguing for tolerance, he is intent on finding something to unify the state. The modern democracies, however, attempt to have pluralism and stability at the same time. Yet even democratic theorists still have concerns whether this attempt can be successful. For example, the central problem in John Rawls's *Political Liberalism* is how a liberal society that is necessarily pluralistic can maintain stability for the right reasons (Rawls 1996). It seems that Han Fei Zi had greater reason to worry. For he saw in his day that a lack of centralized power often led to political chaos, which caused everyone, not just the ruler, to suffer. In fact, this seems to have been a justified concern throughout Chinese history, and indeed much of the history of the rest of the civilized world. One reason contemporary states can undergo internal reform while maintaining a plural and stable system may well be that they are able to exert control over every person and every corner of the territory much more effectively[13] than dreamed of by Han Fei Zi, thanks to technological advance.[14] If this is indeed the case, then his reasoning on the question of stability is both confuted and upheld.

Han Fei Zi was concerned exclusively with maintaining the absolute authority of the ruler. To this end, it was inacceptable for ministers to have any share of his power. He argues in Chapter 5 that there are five ways in which a ruler's power can be blocked: the ministers ostracize their ruler; the ministers gain control of the wealth and interests of the state; the ministers issue orders at will; the ministers are able to perform virtuous deeds (meaning that they can grant favours in their own name); and the ministers can recommend and cultivate their own people. 'All these offices should be exercised by the ruler alone, and should never pass into the hands of his ministers' (Chapter 5).

The ideal minister has to obey the ruler absolutely. He has 'no other loyalty' than that to his ruler.

> He follows the lead of his superior, and obeys the laws of his sovereign. Emptying his mind, he awaits orders and does not question whether they are right or wrong. Thus he has a mouth, but he does not speak for private advantage; he has eyes, but he does not look for private gain; he is fully controlled by his superior.

If a minister is likened to a hand, then even faced with the sharpest sword it would have to sacrifice itself to protect the body. To sum up the teachings, Han Fei Zi quotes a line from an old sage-ruler:

> Ministers shall not wield the instruments of authority nor dispense benefits, but follow the commands of the king. They shall not do evil, but follow the king's path. (Chapter 6)

This appears to be similar to a line in a reputedly older document (Chen 2000: 106). But the latter emphasizes the necessary impartiality of ministers, rather than the absolute obedience emphasized in the *Han Fei Zi*. Han Fei Zi might have been intentionally skewing an old saying to support his point.

The righteous, solitary and indignant man

Between the two passages quoted above, Han Fei Zi lists certain kinds of minister who should not be praised. Other than those already mentioned, he includes 'those who make light of ranks and stipends and are quick to leave the state in order to choose another sovereign' and 'those who propound doctrines through deception and violate laws, and defy their sovereign and forcefully admonish the ruler' (Chapter 6). Those who refuse to serve a bad ruler and leave a state and those who dare to risk their lives to admonish the ruler would be praised by Confucians, but Han Fei Zi did not approve of such behaviour. Indeed, for Han Fei Zi, there may well be some who are not moved by rewards and punishments; yet, instead of praising them, as Confucians would do, he considered them dangerous to the state because they cannot be effectively controlled by the ruler. In Chapter 14, he mentions two noblemen in the past, Bo Yi 伯夷 and Shu Qi 叔齐. They refused to serve the Zhou court because they were loyal to Shang and considered Zhou's takeover illegitimate; instead they chose to run away and starve themselves to death. Although they were praised by Confucians and others for being loyal, Han Fei Zi said they had no merit because 'they were not afraid of heavy punishment, and saw no benefit in substantial rewards. They cannot be deterred by punishment, and cannot be motivated by reward' (Chapter 14).

However, Han Fei Zi himself could not gain the ear of the Han king's, and was instead forced to become a companion to the king of Qin. Being a great patriot, he had a strong desire to change the policies of the state of Han, but he believed that any forceful admonishments would be detrimental to this cause. Again we face the question: when a ruler is not ideal, other than relying on the external check on his power, namely the strength of the state, is it possible from within to alter his behaviour? Han Fei Zi did not support this idea theoretically, and he was quite pessimistic about its practical possibility in his home state. Two chapters in the *Han Fei Zi* address the problems, even dangers, involved in trying to win over a bad ruler: 'Difficulties in Speaking' (Chapter 3), which considers the obstacles to engaging the king in discussion about good policies; and 'Solitary Indignation' (Chapter 11). As his titles suggest, these chapters strongly and vividly convey the anxiety, pain and, indeed, indignation of Han Fei Zi, the great patriot of the state of Han.

Then, in Chapter 12, entitled 'Difficulties in Persuasion', Han Fei Zi offers what appears to be shameless and treacherous advice to those who would have the ear of the king, including manipulation of the ruler to defer to the adviser's will. Some take this as evidence that Han Fei Zi does not pass muster as a theoretical thinker, but was merely a man who tailored his messages to his audience.[15] Yet from his writings as a whole and from the palpable sense of patriotism and desperation conveyed in Chapters 3 and 11, this judgement seems to be problematic. What Han Fei Zi might actually be offering is a way to gain the ear of the king, whereupon one can right the wrongs of the king without jeopardizing the political framework. But if this is the case, how could a person with private ambitions be prevented from using the same artfulness to 'wrong the rights' of a good king or simply usurp his power? Han Fei Zi does not sanction the use of an internal mechanism to inhibit a bad king, and the 'back channel' that he proposes is in practice highly problematic.

An equally serious question is, what in Han Fei Zi's theoretical framework justifies his profound patriotism? Why did he risk all kinds of danger, including getting himself killed, to put the king to rights? Isn't someone like Han Fei Zi, beyond the enticement of direct gain and the vanity of superficial reputation, precisely the kind of person he claims the ruler should get rid of? Perhaps his thinking lacks clarity. Or, more likely, perhaps he did not care to think clearly on this issue. What preoccupied him was gaining the ear of the king of Han, and saving his troubled home state. All his theories are directed towards these goals. As a consequence, however, his theoretical framework reveals fundamental problems and tensions.

SIX

Later developments:
the middle way

We have now considered the three main schools of political philosophy in traditional China, and assessed the historical implications
of certain key ideas. In this chapter, I will offer a more systematic
and intensive discussion of these implications. We will see how ideas
from these schools were put into practice, tried out and incorporated
into the history of politics in traditional China. By noting their successes and failures, we will gain further knowledge of their merits
and shortcomings. Moreover, as discussed in the Introduction and
Chapter 1, and touched on throughout this book, the SAWS were
periods in which China was entering modernity; early traditional
Chinese thought thus constitutes modern philosophy. Subsequent
historical development can thus be viewed as competing political
paradigms of modernity. Therefore, understanding the successes and
failures of these paradigms can also shed light on modernity and
contemporary politics. For the historical account, I will rely heavily
on the works of Qian (1996, 2005), which are in my view two of the
best works on the history of traditional Chinese politics. Interested
readers able to read Chinese should consult them for the detail of
many of the issues discussed in this chapter.

The successes and failures of the Qin dynasty and of Han Fei Zi's teachings

Following policies and political arrangements that Han Fei Zi would have heartily endorsed, the state of Qin unified China, and became the Qin dynasty. Power was centralized. The weapons from the six other strong states were collected and melted down, and the noblemen from these states were moved to the capital of Qin, with the clear intention of monitoring them closely. The jun xian 郡县 system was established throughout the unified country; this involved the Qin emperor appointing the officials of every level, from the provinces (jun) to the counties (xian).[1] Anything that could potentially lead to a rival centre of power was closely watched and designated a danger to be eliminated. Some Qin policies appear to have been lifted from the Han Fei Zi. For example, as we saw in the previous chapter, Han Fei Zi argued that 'there are no letters written on bamboo slips, and laws supply the instruction. There are no sermons of the early kings, and the magistrates serve as the instructors (Chapter 49). Following this faithfully, Qin established a thoroughgoing bureaucracy, or rule by bureaucrats. Books other than those giving practical instruction on agriculture were collected and stored in the imperial court, and were not allowed to be collected by private people. Indeed, the First Emperor was said to have carried out a policy of 'burning books and burying Confucians'. Some argue that this policy was not as sweeping and brutal as it sounds, although it cannot be denied that the texts recovered from Qin dynasty tombs were far less rich and diverse than those from earlier tombs.

The Qin dynasty, under its ambitious and powerful ruler the First Emperor, looked invincible. Indeed, the First Emperor called himself such on the assumption that his descendants would be called simply the Second Emperor, the Third Emperor, and so on for all eternity. Yet, only some fifteen years after its founding, the dynasty collapsed during the reign of the Second Emperor.

Some have argued that this shows the complete non-viability of the Qin (and Legalist) regime. With the following dynasties claiming to follow Confucian teachings, some have further argued that it is clear that it was Confucian political teachings that won the day. However, it is important to see that the changes the Qin dynasty brought about were radical. Radical changes produce radical reactions. The majority of those who rebelled against Qin had or claimed to have connections with the six other states that it had conquered, and wished to restore the lost world of separate states. After the Han dynasty was established, the rulers tried a feudalistic structure mixed with the *jun xian* (province–county) system, enfeoffing the emperor's relatives as independent princes of their fiefdoms, and placing provinces and counties directly under the rule of the central government. But a rebellion by some of these princes led the rulers to realize that this feudalistic structure would not work, and so they went back completely to the *jun xian* system. Under Qin rule, written language, measuring standards, and so forth were unified, which was not the case during the Warring States period; this legacy has remained intact. Indeed, given the major variations among Chinese dialects (which are even greater than those among many European languages), it is hard to imagine that the Chinese people could have held on to the idea of cultural identity through the dynastic changes had the written language not been unified.

In general terms, many essential elements of the Qin regime – centralization of power, bureaucracy, and so on – endured, and became established as central elements of traditional regimes in China. In this sense, there was a strong Legalistic aspect to traditional Chinese politics. The Qin dynasty, moreover, has often been referred to in Chinese history as 'the tyrannical Qin' (*bao Qin* 暴秦); yet, as a passage from Chapter 14 of the *Han Fei Zi*, quoted in the previous chapter, argues, it is precisely in a Legalistic state termed tyrannical that everyone can be prosperous and kind to one another. The Qin dynasty brought to an end hundreds of years of wars in China; and it can safely be said that the policies introduced and the political institutions established served to prevent many brutal killings.

Notwithstanding the above defence, there are fundamental points at issue concerning both the political regime of the Qin dynasty and Han Fei Zi's teachings. Although on rare occasions Han Fei Zi presents his state in terms of a humane ideal, throughout much of the *Han Fei Zi* the strength of the state is the prime concern. Indeed, he argues repeatedly that a concern with humanity and the virtues is something we cannot afford in the age of modernity. As we have seen, he observes that

> Those who do not get their fill of the coarsest grain do not seek fine millet and meat, and those who do not have rags do not expect to have embroidered robes. In dealing with governmental affairs, when you haven't solved the urgent matters, you should not address what is not urgent. (Chapter 49)

But is there a time when non-urgent matters can be addressed? In Chapter 49, he explains how the age has changed from antiquity to modernity, and he seems to take his version of modernity as the end of history. But is there an age beyond the 'end of history'? Han Fei Zi is either denying or being silent about it.

In a sense the change did mark 'the end of history'. By unifying China, the Qin dynasty dissolved all the pressing threats from other states, other than perhaps the nomadic Huns. Instead of savouring the peace and prosperity of its people, it continued to expand its reach. But this expansion brought about new threats, imagined or real. It also continued to launch new grand projects: the Great Wall, the E Fang 阿房 palace, the tomb of the First Emperor, all of which involved exploitation of the people. This eventually led to rebellions, which originated with disgruntled drafted peasant soldiers. Arguably the First Emperor was too ambitious, the task of establishing a new political order too daunting. Yet the fact that Han Fei Zi's political theory contained no warning against the danger of expansionist policies and offered no vision for 'the time after the end of history' might be seen as responsible theoretically for Qin's eventual demise.

Moreover, in the process of centralizing power, Han Fei Zi did not allow ministers any freedom of deliberation. His worries were justifiable. Ruthless or ambitious ministers could well take advantage of any latitude to appropriate power from the central government, and eventually weaken the state. This threat is even more palpable if the state is large and its furthest reaches cannot be effectively controlled. However, when a state is large, its affairs become far too complicated for the central authority or established laws and institutions to anticipate, and this demands that a degree of flexibility be granted to local ministers. Indeed, the aforementioned peasant-soldier revolt began when the draftees travelling to their posts in the frontiers were stopped by unexpected heavy rain. According to the laws of Qin, if drafted peasants failed to reach their posts in time, they faced execution. So, realizing that they would die anyway, some peasants decided to rebel, for at worst they would be executed, which was no different from the fate that awaited them if they chose to be obedient.

This identifies another problem with Han Fei Zi's system. If regulation of the people relies exclusively on a system of rewards and punishments, this will cease to be effective when there is nothing left to give (in terms of reward) or to take away (in terms of punishment). We can already see the deficiency of punishment in the peasant uprising that triggered the spate of rebellions that brought down the mighty Qin dynasty. Similarly, someone doing well according to the legal and institutional requirements will be promoted; but rewards may become less appealing when they follow one after the other, as the law of diminishing marginal utility dictates. Even more to the point, when an official is finally promoted to the very top position within the state, second only to the emperor, there is nowhere higher for him to go. So the emperor will then become worried, and must find ways of demoting or getting rid of him. When the emperor takes this course of action in instances when the top official has done no wrong according to the law, the impartiality of the reward and punishment system breaks down. Yet if the emperor does not act, the official might depose him, which did indeed happen on occasion in imperial history.

There are two possible solutions: allow the emperor to be replaced by an official if the latter has done very well or promote moral education that instils a sense of loyalty into officials and a sense of trust in the emperor. Han Fei Zi, however, objects to both solutions. (Confucians would of course welcome them.) This leads to another question regarding Han Fei Zi's system: is it really the case that there is no room for moral values in statecraft, on the grounds that they have no utility and can even be dangerous to the state?

As we have just seen, moral values may in fact be instrumental to the stability of the state. Han Fei Zi argues that moral values are not reliable, and so it seems if we follow his argument. But his great rhetorical skill serves to deceive. It is true that caring mothers may have bad sons, but equally criminals continue to exist under the most stringent legal system. Perhaps, therefore, the most reliable measure is a mixture of laws and moral values. It is also true that sophisticated teachings are not useful to those who wish to regulate the masses. However, as we saw in our discussion of Confucianism, the early Confucians, especially Confucius himself, made it clear that although the higher teachings have no application for people of lesser understanding, there are simpler moral codes that they can understand and follow. Han Fei Zi also argues for the inevitability of a pluralism of values, refusing to allow these values to permeate the public sphere. This argument is echoed in the work of some contemporary liberals. But as we saw in our discussion of Confucianism, early Confucians perceived a continuity between the private and the public. Moreover, many of their values seem to be thin enough to have a degree of universality and can thus function well in the public sphere. For example, regardless of whether one is a Christian, a Buddhist, a Muslim or an atheist, one may consider stability to be a good quality for a state and acknowledge the fact that the stability of the family is instrumental to the stability of the state. In which case, one will believe that values that promote the stability of the family should be encouraged. This understanding can be considered a value in itself, yet it is one that can be endorsed by many people subscribing to different comprehensive doctrines.

The hybrid regime:
laws and institutions with a Confucian foundation

Perhaps perceiving shortcomings in Han Fei Zi's political philosophy (embodied by the Qin regime), and realizing that there could be no return to the feudalistic system following the failed attempt by early Han rulers to have a mixture of the province–county system with the feudal system (see previous section), later Han rulers and politicians decided to try a hybrid regime. Han was founded on the ruins of Qin, and a return to stable conditions was required. So, as we have seen, the first Han rulers adopted a laissez-faire policy, close to that recommended in the *Lao Zi*, thereby 'allowing people to rest'. But the situation of de facto isolated small states did not last for long. With production back on track, commerce and other activities to which the *Lao Zi* would object flourished once again. The Han rulers faced the question of what was the proper regime to administer a large, populous, and relatively well-connected state. The centralization of power, bureaucracy and promotion based upon verifiable results were elements that could not be done away with. Nevertheless Confucian factors were reintroduced into the system.

Han Fei Zi would not have approved of this reintroduction. Indeed, his system did not seem to permit the importation of Confucianism. However, the Legalistic arrangements referred to above could be absorbed by Confucianism. Early Confucians were not keen on discussing institutional arrangements; some might have cherished hopes of going back to the feudalistic regime. But once they had decided to move forward to embrace the new reality, they would be compelled to consider the issue of institutional arrangements. As discussed in earlier chapters, the early Confucians were consciously or unconsciously attending to the problem of modernity. It is true that Mencius discusses little concerning new institutional arrangements; indeed his emphasis on internal moral values might be seen to preclude consideration of external institutional arrangements. However, Xun Zi discusses the significance of institutions extensively, although his focus is on rites, rituals and codes of conduct. For Confucius, in an ideal state, laws and other regulations will be rendered useless. Still, being a keen observer of human reality, he understood that states in the real world fall far short of the ideal. He was not against the use of laws, including rewards and punishments, but insisted that moral values should be the final goal and the basis of institutional organization.

For example, a pupil asks Confucius what would be the first thing to do in a state where there was a fierce struggle for the throne between the father (Kuai Kui 蒯聩) and one of his sons (Duke Chu of Wei 卫出公). Confucius' answer is to 'get the names right' (*zheng ming* 正名). He explains:

> If names are not right, speeches won't be reasonable; if speeches are not reasonable, affairs will not culminate in success; if affairs do not culminate in success, rites and music will not flourish; if rites and music do not flourish, punishments will not be proper; if punishments are not proper, the common people will not know where to put their hands and feet. (*Analects* 13.3)

Thus it is clear that Confucius believes that it is punishments (and rewards) that directly regulate the masses. Yet punishments and rewards should be answerable to something higher, the rightful names or the moral order.

'Getting names right' is a central Confucian teaching. Confucius explains this teaching as implying 'let the ruler be a ruler, the subject a subject, the farther a father, and the son a son' (*Analects* 12.11). That is, the ruler/subject/father/son should do what his title (name) requires him to do. Han Fei Zi seems to share this idea. It might have been be a common reaction to the disorder during the

SAWS when, following the collapse of the old order, a lot of people were trying to usurp power that did not rightfully belong to them. But Confucians associate titles with moral duties, while Han Fei Zi firmly objects to this association. Elsewhere, Confucius says:

> Guide them by edicts, keep them in line with punishments, and the masses will be saved [from getting into trouble] but will have no sense of shame. Guide them by virtue, keep them in line with rites, and they will have a sense of shame and will obey willingly. (*Analects* 2.3)

Thus, for Confucius, it is important for people to have some moral sense that will provide a firm foundation for legal arrangements. Otherwise rewards and punishments are built upon sand, and the grand edifice will fall in spite of its apparent invincibility, just as happened to the Qin dynasty.

After some fierce struggles, advanced and promoted by the important Han Confucian Dong Zhongshu 董仲舒 (179–104 BCE), Emperor Wu of Han 汉武帝 ordered that the state 'abolish the hundred schools, and respect Confucianism alone' – 'respect' in the sense of taking Confucianism as the state ideology. But, as we have seen, Confucians are able to assimilate a number of Legalistic arrangements. For example, bureaucracy would stay, but Confucians would try to pack it with those possessing Confucian merits. Ideally, people with Confucian merits would be identified by determining whether they were endowed with an inner sense of morality. But this cannot be done when the state is large and populous, at which point a procedure based upon easily verifiable external results has to be established. Such a procedure departs from both the Confucian idea and that of Han Fei Zi to form a combination of the two.

Confucian attempts to check the ruler

The Confucians did not give up their hope that even the ruler himself could be replaced by someone truly worthy. This addresses another fundamental problem with Han Fei Zi's system, the irreplaceability of a non-ideal ruler. They succeeded to an extent: an ambitious minister of the Han dynasty, Wang Mang 王莽, did take this idea to heart, and, believing that he was the chosen one, took the throne and started 'The New Dynasty.' Unfortunately, though, Wang Mang and his New Dynasty proved to be a political failure. He ended the Former Han (also known as the Western Han) dynasty, but his own was soon overturned. The Eastern Han was finally established by an individual of the Han royal blood line.

This failure was a major blow to the Confucians, but they did not give up. Instead of trying to do away with the hereditary throne in favour of rule by the worthy, they moved to strengthen the political voice of Confucians in the imperial court. The early Confucians tried to humanize the divine, offering a humanistic interpretation of heavenly will; the Han Confucians, however, apparently made heaven less human and more divine again. But rather than this being a retreat to the pre-Confucian status quo ante, by elevating heaven's role in political matters, and with their de facto monopoly on interpreting heavenly will, the Han Confucians may have been manoeuvring to 'steal' power from the emperor.

Later, during the Tang (618–907 CE) and Song (960–1279 CE) dynasties, two strong dynasties after the Han, and especially during the Northern Song dynasty (960–1127 CE), the authority of the emperor was checked by the powerful office of the prime minister and by other scholar-officials; hence the empire was de facto co-ruled by the emperor and these officials, at least during certain periods. For example, decrees issued by the emperor alone, without the approval of certain offices controlled by scholar-officials, would not translate into state edicts. Confucian thinkers and politicians also advanced the ideas of the Authority of Governance (zhi tong 治统) and the Authority of the Way (dao tong 道统). He who actually holds the most power in government, the emperor, possesses the Authority of Governance, but it is those endowed with the Authority of the Way who should run the state. The ideal situation is identity between these authorities (he who has the actual authority, 'the Authority of Governance,' is also the one who has the moral authority, 'the Authority of the Way'). But when this is not the case the ruler should at least yield some power to those who have the moral authority. This represents the theoretical basis for the bold tenet of Confucians that the emperor and scholar-officials should co-rule the state. The late Ming and early Qing thinker Huang Zongxi 黄宗羲 (1610–1695) in his Ming Yi Dai Fang Lu 明夷待访录 was more discrediting of the role of emperor, arguing in favour of clearly separating the emperor from the state, and for greater political power to be wielded by the scholar-officials.

In addition to proposing institutional arrangements and providing their theoretical underpinning, Confucians also exerted their influence through the education of the 'crown prince' who was on his way to becoming the next emperor. Moreover, due partly to the failure of certain political reforms during the early part of the Northern Song, Confucian scholars in the late Northern Song, Southern Song (1127–1279) and Ming (1368–1644) dynasties also saw the limitations in the ideal that emperor and scholar-officials should co-rule the state and have responsibility for the education of the next emperor. Instead of, or in addition to, 'gaining the emperor's ear so as to practise the Way' (de jun xing dao 得君行道), these Confucians tried to 'enlighten the people so as to practise the Way' (jue min xing dao 觉民行道). They established private schools, and cultivated the village gentry (xiang shen 乡绅), trying to make the latter de facto magistrates of local affairs and to render local communities autonomous.

Such arrangements lasted until the time China was forced into confrontation with the West, the first significant instance of which is the First Opium War, 1839–1842, when the British tried to protect their sale of opium to China with gunboats.[2] Since that time, traditional political and social structures have collapsed due to successive government failures, the importation of Western ideas and deliberate destruction by Chinese radicals (the first generation of Chinese Communists being the most radical), and, lately, thirty-plus years of rapid capitalization and development of a market and industrialized economy. This economy changed the agriculture-based economy of traditional China, and thereby also destroyed the social structure on the basis of which Confucians built their cultural influence. It follows that the Confucian revival among small circles of devoted Chinese, especially academics, could only have a meaningful influence if it was able to reinvent a Confucian social and political structure that complemented what is now an industrialized and mobile society.

Selection of the worthy

With regard to the best means to select the worthy for high office, traditional Chinese thinkers and politicians post-Qin put a variety of procedures to the test. The Han dynasty adopted the policy of 'recommending the filial and the upright' (ju xiao lian 举孝廉), whereby those in local government possessing these qualities were recommended for service in central government. This worked alongside the Imperial College (tai xue 太学) system: promising young students attended an Imperial College; those who did well would be given positions in local government; those who stood out were selected, through the institution of 'recommending the filial and the upright', for positions in central government and sent back to the capital.

Gradually, though, this system became the de facto monopoly of a few established clans (shi zu 世族). They were rich and powerful, and their children had access to a good education and to employment in the bureaucracy. Although it was not required that the elite come from these clans, people from or associated with them were dominant in the ruling class. The Tang dynasty witnessed a transition from this system to one that was more open to the best and brightest from families with no connections. This change was partly due to the fact that the big clans were devastated in the seemingly endless chaos following the collapse of the Han dynasty. The ke ju 科举 system, sometimes translated as the Chinese civil service exam system (although this translation is somewhat misleading as those selected are often not merely civil servants, but members of the ruling structure), was then established: students could get a ticket to the high-level bureaucracy (county magistrate and above) by taking written exams. Some Confucians deplored this change, considering excellence in these exams unrelated to the worthiness of an individual, especially during the Ming and Qing (1644–1911) dynasties, when the exams were based upon rather formulaic subject matter (*ba gu wen* 八股文). But, as discussed, the inner worth of an individual is a quality impossible to determine in a large and populous state, and so external criteria had to be brought into the equation, as Han Fei Zi argues.

In spite of the reservations of some Confucians, the Chinese civil service exams, or *ke ju*, offered better opportunities to those with no connections, and thus encouraged greater upward mobility. But there was a price to pay. As we saw, in the period between the Han and early Tang dynasties, people from established clans came to dominate the upper echelon of politics, at the expense of the disadvantaged and disenfranchised. But they tended to be very well educated, and had a close knowledge of politics. As a consequence, they tended to be politically savvy and know the boundaries. Those members of the elite inducted through civil service exams, however, lacked such exposure, and therefore tended to be politically naive and sometimes ruthless.[3]

Interestingly, a similar change and contrast may have occurred in American political history, according to the evaluation of the political observer David Brooks. He argues (Brooks 2010) that fifty or more years ago the upper echelon of American society and politics was dominated by the 'Protestant Establishment' or the 'Power Elite', while American society today is considerably more upwardly mobile and thus more meritocratic. Apparently, then, contemporary society is fairer, but there is also a price to pay. First, according to Brooks, the criteria of merit are too narrow, focusing on the ability to amass technical knowledge and not on sensitivity to context and a sense of empathy. But a political leader needs to be able to make sensible decisions based upon various contextual factors and to be compassionate towards those he or she leads. Thus today's meritocracy is not in very good shape. Second, those from the established families, because they had connections with each other, tended to know the extent to which they could persecute other politicians from the same background. Hence political friction was not as ugly as it is today. Third, and relatedly, due to their deep-rooted and durable background and connections, those from established families tended to have long-term concerns, in contrast to the more 'individualistic' and self-interested (in the narrow sense) politics of today.

Following the same logic, one might ponder the present political situation in China. There is by all accounts a struggle ongoing in contemporary Chinese politics between the *tuan pai* 团派 (officials who started out as leaders of the Chinese Communist Youth League, including the current president Hu Jintao) and the *tai zi dang* 太子党 ('princelings', whose older relatives were founders of Communist China). One argument in favour of the legitimacy of the princelings' power and their superiority over those with no political background is precisely that presented above. But it is perhaps debatable whether their families are as educated and deeply rooted as traditional powerful Chinese families or 'blue blood' American families were.

Centralization of power versus local autonomy

Another important issue for traditional Chinese politics was the balance between centralized power and local autonomy. As we saw, a problem with Han Fei Zi's system and with the Qin regime was overcentralization of power. In a large and populous state, flexibility is necessary, and local officials need a degree of autonomy to respond to particular problems. The balance between centralization and autonomy was often expressed in the history of traditional Chinese political thought through the relations between the *jun xian* system and feudalism. For feudalism allowed a considerable degree of autonomy to be given to local governments. Early Confucians might appear to have been fond of the Zhou feudal system, and they believed in the human capacity to make good decisions. Thus they tended to emphasize the importance of feudalistic arrangements. But clearly later Chinese thinkers saw that there could be no return to feudalism, but some argued for a healthy blend of jun xian centralization and feudal autonomy.[4]

In the Han dynasty, the central government controlled provincial posts but ceded much autonomy to lower-level officials. However, to maintain a shared sense of unity, these officials could be promoted or transferred freely to the central government. This was an attempt to allow some autonomy without risking disunity. But when channels between the central and local governments became congested, this balance was threatened. Indeed, the Han and Tang dynasties, which allowed local governments more autonomy, were plagued by the problem of disunity, and were eventually brought down by factious provincial officials behaving like feudal lords. The governments of the Song and Ming dynasties were more centralized, but their problem lay with a lack of flexibility at the local level.[5]

Bad blends of Legalism and Confucianism

Thus, generally speaking, traditional Chinese regimes after Qin were a mixture of the Legalist and Confucian systems, which were largely complementary. Some conspiracy theorists like to characterize these regimes as being Confucian on the outside and Legalist on the inside (yang ru yin fa 阳儒阴法), but I consider this to be misreading. There were, however, some bad blends of the two systems. For example, through the theory of Yin and Yang by Dong Zhongshu – in which the ruler, the father and the husband are associated with the dominant Yang, while the minister, the son and the wife are associated with the submissive Yin (Chun Qiu Fan Lu 春秋繁露, Volume 12) – the famous tenet of 'three bonds/cardinal guides' was developed, which was to be considered Confucian orthodoxy (Bai Hu Tong Yi 白虎通义, Volume 7). This dictates that, in a dominant manner, the ruler guides the minister, the father guides the son, and the man guides the wife. The mutual familial care of early Confucians becomes a one-directional relationship of obedience and loyalty. The Confucian idea of the centrality of family is deployed to bolster the authority of the ruler. It was in fact Han Fei Zi who first introduced this idea:

> The minister serves the ruler; the son serves the father; the wife serves the husband. If these three principles are followed, the world will be in order. If the three principles are violated, the world will be in chaos. (*Han Fei Zi* Chapter 51)[6]

Here, the Confucian duty-based hierarchy (the higher up the political ladder, the greater the duty) degenerates into an oppressive one.

Let us consider another example of a bad blend of systems. As we saw, Han Fei Zi wanted central government to have total control over people's political actions by way of laws and institutions. He had little concern for people's intentions and motivations. Confucians, especially those in Mencius's tradition, did care about intentions, but Mencius wouldn't support the use of oppressive power to achieve the elevation of morality. The combining of Han Fei Zi's idea of state control and Mencius's belief in the importance of thought (ignoring both Han Fei Zi's lack of concern for thought and Mencius's emphasis on self-motivation as the key to becoming a moral person) produced a true totalitarianism intended to control not only people's behaviour but also their thinking. Thus in traditional China, especially during the last Manchurian dynasty, the Qing, there were persecutions, wen zi yu (文字獄, persecutions based upon one's writings), that were based upon people's speeches and writings. For they could be interpreted, or, more precisely, distorted, into something that was considered treacherous. A reason for this totalitarian control, which may not have been the norm in traditional Chinese politics, is that the Manchurian dynasty was founded by an alien minority group that subsequently tried to control the non-Manchurian Chinese majority.[7] Interestingly, a similar system of thought control was instituted during the Cultural Revolution, when an alien ideology, communism, was utilized in order to wield total control over the Chinese people. A famous slogan during the Cultural Revolution was

'Fight hard against even a fleeting spark of private [interest]' (狠斗 私字一闪念). To be clear, neither Han Fei Zi nor Mencius, on the basis of their own theories, would have supported this degree of totalitarian control.

China: an authoritarian state?

It is quite common for China, in both its traditional and its contemporary form, to be referred to as an 'authoritarian state'. We saw in the previous section that one blend of Confucianism and Legalism produced a thoroughgoing instance of totalitarian control. But this form of regime was the exception rather than the rule in traditional Chinese politics.

Whereas it is true that Han Fei Zi's own thoughts came close to authoritarianism, we note that many of his concerns and endeavours have either been shared by modern Western thinkers or were motivated by reasonable concerns at the time. Moreover, his theory in point of fact posited an ideal state in which the ruler as an individual disappears, to be immersed in and identified with the state. Unfortunately, the emperors in late dynasties did not constitute Han Fei Zi's faceless embodiment of the Way, being to some extent authoritarian rulers. However, as we have seen in this chapter, Confucians attempted to curb their power through various means. After failing to remodel the throne as an office based on merit, they tried to limit the power of the emperor by instructing the crown prince, educating both the masses and the gentry, strengthening the office of scholar-official, and sustaining local autonomy.

One crucial achievement of Confucian education was the grounding of the sovereign's legitimacy in the well-being and satisfaction of the people. For the Chinese, the state has to function for the people in order to be legitimate. By contrast, for example, Alexander the Great is said to have conquered the world exclusively in the pursuit of glory, and as such tends to be considered a heroic figure in the West. This perspective is hardly imaginable for the Chinese. In the

non-Chinese world, generally speaking, there are regimes that have
tended to pursue goals based on the private interests of a narrow
group (the king, the king's family, the ruling minority), or on a
'common good' that Chinese consider not to be part of people's
interest, such as heavenly reward in the case of the Crusaders. Even
the Chinese Communists in the first thirty years of their rule (when
China was actually communist, in contrast to the last thirty or more
years, during which the country has been communist in name only)
had to justify their rule in the name of 'serving the people' 为人民
服务. This understanding of legitimacy, then, leaves the door open
for people to challenge a government on the grounds that it fails
to serve the people. This offers another check on the authority of
the government.

   Failure to understand this deeply rooted sense of legitimacy and
its effect in Chinese politics – for example, the present Chinese
government is highly conscious of the need to serve the people in
order to justify its rule – may be a key reason why many China
observers misjudge the capacity of the present administration to
survive. For they characterize it as a purely oppressive regime that
disregards people's interests, in common with many other authoritarian states in the world. It may be the case that some leaders in
the Chinese government share with Western observers the notion
that the administration is unstable, failing to appreciate the crucial
differences between China and the autocratic regimes that have been
overturned in recent history (the Arab Spring being the most recent
example).[8] The tendency to overreaction and increased oppression
by the Chinese government point to this misunderstanding and
explain the sense of insecurity that is manifest. However, if we
take a closer look at the real world, for example the Arab states, the
wealth is in most cases concentrated in the hands of the ruling class
(be it the king and his extended family or a small minority within
the state), rather than being widely shared by all. In spite of the
injustices and corruption, when compared to the Arab world and
many African countries, the masses in China share to a reasonable

degree the wealth in the booming economy. A telling joke explains this difference well. A Chinese official opens a window of his new mansion, points to a newly built grand stadium and tells his visitor that this project is the reason he has his mansion (because he appropriated some of the money). An African official similarly opens a window of his new mansion, points to a large area of empty land that was the intended site of a stadium and tells his visitor that the vacant plot is the reason he has his mansion (the stadium has not been built because he stole all the money).

Thus, failure to understand that China's past and present regimes have never been purely authoritarian, thanks largely to Confucian factors, can lead to fundamental misunderstandings about the country and the passing of invalid judgements on China's and the world's future. Such miscalculations by both Westerners and Chinese officials regarding the strength of the Chinese government comes partly from the failure to understand the nature of traditional Chinese regimes. In the past this failure has produced some very unfortunate consequences. As indicated, the last dynasty, the Qing, was established by invaders of a different ethnicity. To strengthen their rule, they stiffened the authoritarian elements of the traditional Chinese regime. China was subsequently defeated first by Western imperialists and then by the Japanese. Chinese intellectuals mistook the weakest moment of this abnormal dynasty as representing the core of traditional Chinese politics, and misguidedly turned their fire on tradition.[9] During the May Fourth Movement (in 1919), Chinese radicals called for the demolition of the 'Confucian Store' (孔家店). The sad irony was that, in their bid to get rid of the authoritarian elements in Chinese politics, they helped to dissolve the Confucian elements that served historically as the main counterbalance. In consequence, Chinese politics has since developed an even more authoritarian tendency, which has reinforced the radicals' conviction that traditional Chinese politics was purely authoritarian. For example, under early Communist rule (Chinese Communists belonged to the most radical wing of the May Fourth Movement), even village officials were directly appointed by the central government. However, throughout much of Chinese history, communities below county level had often enjoyed a large degree of autonomy. Recently China has experimented with village elections, which many Chinese and Westerners welcome as a sign of the country's democratization. Yet this development can equally be viewed as a return to traditional politics, when the regime was far less authoritarian. Generally speaking, there is a tendency to neglect the perspective that strives to understand the present Chinese government by situating it within the history and world-view of traditional Chinese politics, in favour of merely drawing comparisons with non-Chinese politics.[10]

The contemporary relevance of traditional Chinese political philosophy

In framing the problems experienced by early Chinese political thinkers as issues of modernity, explaining the ideas that inform the three main schools of traditional Chinese philosophy and their critical and complementary engagements with each other, and examining their historical and theoretical implications, we are able to appreciate that traditional Chinese political philosophy not only helps us understand China's past and present, but is pertinent to our reflections on contemporary global politics. Many of the implications for our times have already been touched on. In this concluding chapter I will discuss in a more systematic and synthesizing manner the lasting relevance of traditional Chinese political philosophy to today's world.

Understanding modernity

The premiss of this study is that the issues addressed in traditional Chinese philosophy, from its very beginning, are similar to many of the problems experienced in Western modernity. Thus the schools of thought and the political regimes of traditional China offer competing paradigms to help us understand and deal with modernity, and represent a rich resource for improving contemporary politics.

As we have seen, many characteristics of the process of European modernization, which is often taken as the only path to modernity, can be found in the practices and theories of traditional China. The similarities and differences between the two transitions can help us grasp the essence of modernity. Many features considered central to modernity, such as liberty, equality, pluralism, the market economy, plebianization of the military, and so on, should be understood as the consequences of deeper changes: the collapse of feudalism and inherited nobility and the emergence of large, populous, well-connected and mobile states of strangers. The comparison and contrast between China's early modernity and the European process can also help us identify which features are not even secondary but purely contingent. For example, although the emergence of a new kind of sovereign legitimacy (based on the satisfaction of the people) from the old model (based on the divine right of the ruler) is common to China's early modernity and European modernity, the fact that Christianity and the Church were a powerful force in Europe meant that secularization was a far more salient feature there.

I accept that my thesis regarding China's early modernity is a bold one, which invites many objections. Some of these I attempted to pre-empt and answer in Chapter 1. I acknowledge the possibility that European modernization has particular characteristics that are essential to today's world. But I would argue that we can only discover them if we broaden our vision and accept that many features that we had thought were essential to and unique in European modernity are actually not. Let us consider one possible objection to my thesis regarding Chinese modernity. I have contended that a society of strangers emerged during the SAWS, which led to Confucians designating compassion a core value in their political philosophy. But it has been argued that in fact traditional China was a society of acquaintances,[1] which calls my thesis into question. In traditional Chinese agrarian society, local communities were indeed often composed of extended families and acquaintances. However, members of the governing class had to rule over people who were strangers to them, unlike in the case of feudalism, where the pyramid-like structure meant that at each level ruler and ruled could know each other personally; this new social reality made way for compassion to be the agent that enabled relations between strangers (officials and subjects). Yet, although officials could live in cities, their economic base was still in rural areas – that is, in communities of the familiar. Thus the society of strangers in traditional China was perhaps not fully fledged. However, the industrialization that was unique to European modernization changed this pattern in the West: rural areas were no longer the primary economic base; industrialization caused the labour force to migrate, uprooting the masses from their rural roots. This can be taken as a 2.0 version of China's transitions during the SAWS. Hence, the difference between traditional Chinese society and modern European society is not that between a society of acquaintances and a society of strangers, but between an underdeveloped society of strangers and a fully fledged society of strangers.

Another unique feature of European modernity, arguably, is the phenomenon of full-scale mass education. Early Confucians advocated a form of mass education, but in traditional China the state was never able to offer it on the scale we enjoy today. At best, the state established selection criteria of merit that would encourage families to educate their young in order for them to become members of the ruling class. The state therefore didn't have to invest heavily in the kind of schools we have today, but, on the other hand, although it did achieve some success in encouraging education, it fell far short of the scale of mass education introduced over the last two hundred years in the West.[2]

If these two features are indeed developments unique to European modernization and to today's world, the question arises as to whether they have brought about new problems, different from those experienced in the first version of modernity, the Chinese model. For one thing, the two features combined have, I believe, created a pluralism not just among the elite, as was the case in traditional China, but also among the masses. What are the implications of this? We can begin to tackle such questions by careful consideration and extension of the thesis in this book. Even if certain features are deemed to be exclusive to today's world, I believe the commonalities between the contemporary global reality (informed as it has been by European modernization) and traditional China are sufficiently pronounced for the learning obtained from the latter to be beneficial to our greater understanding.

The Confucian middle way: compassion and the hybrid regime

We saw in Chapter 2 that early Confucians introduced the ideas of humanity and compassion as the new social glue. Their key feature was the attempt to achieve a universal yet unequal or hierarchical love. This enables the defining of a middle ground between two extremes on many issues, such as international relations, just war theory, animal rights, feminism, and so on. In Chapter 3, the Confucian middle-way approach was applied to the issue of equality. Early Confucians tried to meld equality with hierarchy, and social mobility with stability. If they could witness today's politics, they would doubtless propose a hybrid regime that combines popular, democratic elements with meritocratic features. As I have argued, such a regime might well address the problems that are fundamentally unresolvable within the framework of liberal democracy. As discussed in Chapter 6, China's past saw experiments in the process of selecting meritocrats and using them to balance other political forces, most importantly the power of the emperor, and in this there were successes and failures, merits and demerits. These lessons can offer us clues when we ponder the issue of how to institutionalize the ideal hybrid regime.

Limits of humans

In our discussion of the political ideas of the *Lao Zi*, we saw forceful attacks on Confucian political philosophy. In particular, it cautions us against human hubris: that is, our belief in our own ability to produce the outcomes we desire. Nature is not necessarily kind to us, and it is beyond human control. We may express pride in our achievements, thinking that they bring us a better world. But we may also fail to realize that these achievements have a dark side that will haunt us. How many such follies have we committed, and do we ever learn? We invented DDT to kill insects and mosquitoes, and then discovered that birds such as the American bald eagle were destroyed by it. As a consequence, many countries decided to ban its use. However, this in turn has apparently led to a rise in deaths due to malaria (Kristof 2005).

Romantics, hippies, new-age people and some environmentalists may embrace the message in the *Lao Zi*. But it should be clear to those people who wish to cure social sickness by human effort, the *Lao Zi* may at once be at odds with them. For, according to the *Lao Zi*, our determination to cure social ills is itself an expression of hubris, which the *Lao Zi* condemns; the effort may only end up perpetuating the ills it intends to cure. As we saw in the final section of Chapter 4, the *Lao Zi* (as well as *Han Fei Zi*) seems not to believe that we can educate the masses into moderating their desires. In which case, the only viable solution is to take temptation away from the masses. But the only effective way to achieve this would be to revert to a situation in which states are small and lightly populated, technologically backward and isolated. This message may not best please the romantic individualists.

Clearly, fundamental obstacles prevent the world ever returning to the state desired by the *Lao Zi*. But this doesn't mean that we can't take its teachings as a cautionary tale. More importantly, in the *Lao Zi* and in the *Han Fei Zi*, the idea is introduced that the natural laws of politics are far more powerful than human effort, and we should thus follow the laws of nature instead of investing human effort that is alien to them. This idea resonates with the contemporary economic notion of the 'invisible hand' of the market and those who caution against government intervention. But then there are those who believe in the benefits of human intervention, as early Confucians did. Thus it is that the dispute between Confucians and the *Lao* Zi (and the *Han Fei Zi*) regarding the active role of humans in politics must be seen as part of a universal and enduring philosophical dialogue. Our investigations into this dispute are therefore also perennial.

Han Fei Zi and modernity

Among the early Chinese political thinkers, Han Fei Zi was perhaps most conscious of the fundamental changes brought about during the SAWS, and in this sense can be seen as the first modern political philosopher. His vision of a depersonalized bureaucracy influenced traditional Chinese politics and anticipated the practice of modern European states. Many of his arguments also looked forward to the arguments of modern European and contemporary thinkers. He offered what was perhaps the first argument for the inevitability of a pluralism of values (in the absence of oppression), although he did not go down the road of tolerance, as many modern European and contemporary thinkers have done. Yet, as we saw, he harboured legitimate worries about the stability of the state in a context of plural values. The fact that we can enjoy both stability and plural-ism today seems to refute Han Fei Zi's ideas, but, as argued, it may be that we have to be able to exert effective control before we can allow tolerance. This message (liberal tolerance presupposes effective control) might appear negative, but it can lead to desirable consequences. Theoretically, this can deepen our understanding of pluralism. Practically speaking, this can help governments that reject tolerance accept that their concern with stability, though legitimate, can be addressed without using oppressive governmental force, especially given today's technology and for a government whose legitimacy derives from the people. That is to say, if a state is effectively controlled, pluralism won't lead to instability. On the other hand, the rejection of pluralism and suppression of any form of popular elections might well do so.

Another issue raised by Han Fei Zi is the relations between the private and the public. Confucians consider these two realms as inhabiting a continuous dimension, but Han Fei Zi focused on the conflict between them. Related to the issue of pluralism, Han Fei Zi wanted to push values back into the private sphere, and only allow into the public sphere what was universal. Contemporary thinkers also tend to focus on the conflict between the two, and seek to separate the public sphere from the private. Of course, unlike Han Fei Zi, by doing so they wish to protect the private realm. However, as has been argued, Confucians may think that there are values 'thin' enough that they can become widely shared public values, which are important for the common good. This may serve as a means to reintroduce values into the public arena, in contrast to today's tendency to evade the issue of social morality, in the name of not imposing the mores of one group of people on everyone.

Competition and convergence

In our discussion of later developments, we saw that ideas of traditional Chinese political philosophy competed and converged, which became a source of liveliness in traditional Chinese politics. We also saw that political ideas from China inspired political thinkers in East Asia and in Europe. The West has largely grown too complacent to see this, or to consider the possibility of it happening again. Dazzled by the achievements of the West, many non-Westerners have also come to the conclusion that the Western way is the only way to go, pointing to the end of history. This complacency and overwhelming sense of awe arguably represents ignorance of the worst kind: being unaware of one's own ignorance gives the ignorant no motive to learn. So perhaps it is time for us to look closely at traditional Chinese political philosophy, in order to understand the self and the present by understanding the other and the past, that we might lead ourselves to a better self and a better future.

Notes

INTRODUCTION

1. A large number of people and works uphold the revive–revenge reading of China, and an equally large number of other people and works believe that China (in its past and present incarnations as well as in terms of its past and present values) offers constructive economic and political alternatives. To offer a comprehensive survey would in itself represent a difficult yet important scholarly undertaking. When discussing detailed issues in this book my practice is to refer to only a few directly relevant works. Interested readers may wish to begin with Bell 2006 and 2008, which are very readable and insightful, and cover much of the recent literature. Another good starting point is works by Weiming Tu 杜维明, a leading authority on the Confucian revival. See his edited volume (1996) with discussions of the role of Confucian values in the rise of Japan and the four 'mini-dragons' in Asia. More recently, Henry Kissinger, one of the most influential diplomats and a keen political observer of the contemporary world, published a book on China; it is a must-read for those who wish to understand China and the various positions held on the country (Kissinger 2011).
2. Nisbett 2003 is perhaps the most influential work on the differences in Western and East Asian patterns of thinking. Works by the late political scientist Tianjian Shi 史天健, in particular 2010 and 2011, show the differential perceptions of certain democratic ideas held by East Asians and Westerners.
3. The numbering of the *Analects* (and the *Mencius*) is virtually standard, although there can be a degree of variation depending on the translation.

Unless otherwise stated, the translations of the *Analects* and other Chinese classical texts are mine. The reader may consult Lau 2000 and 2003 for alternative translations of the *Analects* and the *Mencius*. Chan 1963 is perhaps the best anthology of traditional Chinese philosophical texts in English; the translations are generally superb.

4. A cliché one often hears in discussion of comparative studies is that Westerners think in a simplistic, black-and-white, linear manner, while Chinese do not. The irony is that those who make such remarks don't see that their own formulations are precisely black-and-white, simplistic and linear...

5. According to one source, China produced a greater share of the world's total GDP than any other country for much of the twenty centuries up to 1820 (Maddison 2006: 261–3), at which point it still 'produced over 30 percent of world GDP – an amount exceeding the GDP of Western Europe, Eastern Europe, and the United States combined' (Kissinger 2011: 12).

6. For corroboration of this denial in the West, consider how many experts in Chinese philosophy there are in most university philosophy departments: in most mainstream programmes in research universities the number is zero. Most scholars in Western universities who specialize in Chinese philosophy are in departments other than philosophy (such as East Asian Studies, History, etc.) or in philosophy departments that are considered non-mainstream. In China most philosophy departments will have a group of people studying Chinese philosophy. But issues such as whether traditional thought is a philosophy and the legitimacy of Chinese philosophy as a philosophy 中国哲学合法性问题 have haunted philosophers in China since the word 'philosophy' was introduced there.

7. At least parts of the *Xun Zi* and the *Han Fei Zi*, to name just two classical Chinese texts, are exceptions.

8. It should be noted that not all Western philosophical texts are written in the form of treatises. For example, most extant works by Plato are dialogues, and Nietzsche is known for his aphorisms and other poetic yet philosophical writings.

ONE

1. According to Qian Mu (1996: 55–6), these 'barbarians' were not necessarily of different ethnicities. Rather, they were considered barbarians because they didn't lead a settled, agrarian life, and lacked the sophisticated political structure and culture of the Zhou states.

2. The year in which the Spring and Autumn period began is a matter of debate; more so still is the year in which the Warring States period began.

3. The idea that peoples of different states under the Zhou belong together supposedly comes from the Duke of Zhou, a brother of King Wu and a sage-like ruler who helped the young king after King Wu to consolidate his power and maintain and develop the regime of the Western Zhou by, among other means, apparently introducing the idea that 'there is one common lord for the whole world' (天下共主) – meaning the civilized Chinese world.

4. Hui 2005 also argues that there are profound similarities between China during the SAWS and Europe in the period of its early modernity. She further analyses the issue of why China was eventually unified while Europe was not.

5. To call what China experienced during the SAWS an early modernization is a bold claim. However, other works support my thesis. In adddition to Hui (2005), Francis Fukuyama argues that the Qin dynasty (Qin, a strong state during the Warring States period, defeated all the other states, unified China, and established itself as a dynasty) was the first modern state in human history (2011).

6. See Bai 2011 for a more detailed discussion.

7. For a comprehensive account of this issue, see Hobson 2004.

8. Michael Puett has made these points (1998), citing as an example how China was influenced by the outside world during the Bronze and Early Iron Ages.

9. Hobson 2004 is one of the most recent works to consider this issue.

10. Han 2003 argues that Japan's modern capitalism is not really Confucian capitalism, as many believe, and that Japanese modernization was anticipated by the re-examination of Chinese thought during the SAWS, especially its choosing of Legalism over Confucianism. As we will see, Legalism during the SAWS was the school that most firmly embraced modernity, and so it was no accident, then, that this school received a great deal of attention during the Japanese transition to modernity.

11. I say 'might' here because whether or not the important document referred to in the next sentence was from the Western Zhou period is a controversial issue.

12. See Chapter 6 for further discussion.

13. To use a non-philosophical example, in the debate over whether Chinese medicine is a medical science or not, some argue that it is not unique, as some adherents think, but is close to Ancient Greek medicine (implying that Chinese medicine is a medical science, but an outdated and inferior one). A more philosophical example is the comparison of the Han Confucian view that there is a connection between heaven and human beings with a similar religious belief in medieval Europe.

14. Ironically, even Tang Junyi 唐君毅, who is a member of the twentieth-

century New Confucianism 新儒家 that tries to preserve and promote Chinese traditions, makes this claim (1996: 925).

15. Many Chinese scholars who expose themselves to Western philosophy have made this claim on occasion (conferences, private conversations, etc.). Of course, out of envy of the progress in the modern sciences, this progressive view of philosophy has been a feature of many branches of modern Western philosophy, for example logical empiricism and analytical philosophy.

16. Tang Junyi, for example, makes this claim (1996: 925).

17. For Hegel's attitude towards Chinese philosophy, see the section on Chinese philosophy in his *Lectures on the History of Philosophy*. For a free online English translation, see www.marxists.org/reference/archive/hegel/works/hp/hporiental.htm; accessed 29 January 2012. For Weber's view, see his *Religion of China* (1968).

TWO

1. Qin was the state that conquered all the other states, unified China, and turned itself into the first centralized and non-feudal dynasty in Chinese history.

2. Confucianism is a long and complicated tradition, and therefore phrases such as 'the Confucian view' can be simplifying and misleading. In this book, 'Confucian' and its variants often refer to the teachings that can be found in the *Analects* and in the *Mencius*. Although Xun Zi was one of the three most influential pre-Qin Confucians, his influence in later dynasties was not as obvious and significant as Confucius and Mencius. It follows that most of the 'Confucian' passages cited in this book are taken from the *Analects* and the *Mencius*.

3. Confucius himself didn't seem to think that he had founded a new school, but claimed to transmit the classics of the past (*Analects* 7.1). But for the many original contributions listed below, it is not unjustified calling him the founder of the Confucian school.

4. 'Junzi' 君子 literally means 'son of the ruler', and thus originally referred to a member of the nobility. But as was the case with many such terms, Confucians reinterpreted it, ridding the term of the meaning associated with feudal hierarchy and turning it into something purely meritocratic. Confucius is playing with the double meaning of the term *junzi* here. Clearly, a noble man (in the literal sense) shouldn't engage in lowly work (such as a menial job), and it seems that Confucius thought that a 'meritocrat' shouldn't either. Mencius would tease out the hidden meaning of the latter claim in his works, which we will discuss in the next chapter. I will use the transliteration *junzi* when the double meaning is intended, and use the phrase 'exemplary person' to

translate this term when it is clearly intended without any allusion to nobility in the feudal sense.

5. It is not clear to which aspect of Zhou Confucius is referring here; it is only a possibility that the reference is to the Zhou li.

6. 'Inhumane' translates the negation of ren 仁. 'Ren' is another important term that is difficult to translate. It is often translated as 'benevolence', but in Chinese ren sounds exactly the same as the term for 'human' (人). Thus, I will translate the term ren (which can be used as a noun or an adjective) as 'humane' or 'humanity'.

7. The Chinese term for 'the world' is tian xia 天下, which means literally 'under heaven'. It is sometimes translated as 'all in the world'.

8. 'Mencius' is the Latinized form of 'Meng Zi' – 'Master Meng'. Mencius is said to have studied with a grandson of Confucius, and was a leading scholar in an 'academy' supported by the king of the state of Qi, a powerful state in the Warring States period. He had communicated with a few kings, but wasn't taken seriously enough to be put in any meaningful position.

9. The word for 'compassion' is translated in the previous line as 'the feeling of alarm and distress'. 'The feeling of alarm and distress' is the original meaning of this term (ce yin zhi xin 恻隐之心), which, perhaps thanks to Mencius, is later used to refer to compassion.

10. 'Realistic utopia' is a term that John Rawls coined in his later writings (1999).

11. The translation is mine. For the Chinese version, see Zhang 1978: 62–3. For another English translation, see Chan 1969: 497–8; also Bryan Van Norden's translation at http://faculty.vassar.edu/brvannor/Phil210/Translations/Western%20Inscription.pdf; accessed 20 August 2011.

12. See Analects 2.3, 12.9, 13.3 and 13.6; and Great Learning, ch. 4.

13. For a more detailed discussion of the Confucian ideas of mutual concealment and graded love, see Bai 2008b.

14. Of course, there are differences among these nation-states regarding the meaning of nationalities, and there are clear exceptions such as the United States of America.

15. See, for example, Shapiro 1984; Pollak 1998; Xu 2003. For an online account, see: http://en.wikipedia.org/wiki/Kaifeng_Jews; accessed 16 February 2012.

16. This is a fairly common reading of Chinese history, but recent scholarly works challenge this relatively peaceful image of traditional China. See, for example, Wang 2011; Johnston 1998.

17. Of course the shameful elimination of most Native Americans greatly helped solve the unity problem for the USA.

18. This welcoming scene by the people was mentioned twice more in the

Mencius, when Mencius discusses just wars of liberation (*Mencius* 1B11, where the event described in 1B10 is discussed; and 3B5).

19. That the welcome has to be long-lasting is implied by the last line of the quotation from *Mencius* 1B10. Daniel Bell also argues for the importance of this condition to Mencius's justification of aggressive wars (Bell 2006: 39).

20. A similar passage can be found in 7B4.

21. 1B11 contains a passage similar to the whole passage quoted here.

22. Zhou's reply in Chinese, 与自家意思一般, is not easy to understand and decipher; my translation is based upon one possible reading of it.

23. For a more detailed discussion, see Bai 2009a and 2009b: ch. 4.

24. Again, for a more elaborate account and for the discussion of other relevant issues, see Bai 2009a and 2009b: ch. 4.

25. We do not know if most of the views expressed by the character Socrates in the Platonic dialogues are those of the historical individual Socrates. Since Plato never speaks in any of his own dialogues, we cannot be sure if any of the views expressed there are those of Plato. Thus I can only safely say that the character Socrates in this or that dialogue of Plato has this or that view.

26. It is true that men are now more involved in child-rearing, but pregnancy, giving birth and (to a lesser extent) breastfeeding are still burdens women *have to* assume (which is not to deny that men can, by choice, play an assisting role).

27. Other recent attempts to address the issue of Confucianism and feminism are, for example, Chan 2003; Li 2000; Wang 2003.

THREE

1. A passage in the *Analects* (6.19) was sometimes interpreted as Confucius claiming the innate goodness of human nature, although many disagreed with this interpretation. Those who interpreted it thus were leading Neo-Confucians, who were heavily influenced by Mencius. This renders their interpretation suspect. See Cheng 1990: 402–3.

2. The term *shi* 士 referred to an official in the feudal system who was of noble pedigree. Later, thanks to the early Confucian reinterpretation of the old system, it referred to Confucian intellectuals and scholar-officials, among others.

3. As we have seen, Mencius believes that everyone can be good if he or she chooses to do so. Thus the criminal is accountable also for his or her criminal deeds.

4. The art of claiming one's heritage might have been a part of a 'pissing contest' among pre-Qin schools of thought. Most schools, especially those that believed antiquity to be superior to the present time, thought

that the longer their thought could go back in history the more credible it was. Shen Nong was said to be someone living in an earlier time than Yao and Shun, the Confucian heroes.

5. See Bell 2008: 38–55 for a similar but more elaborate discussion.

6. For example, Gan Yang 甘阳, an influential contemporary public intellectual in China, has made this claim (2007). However, I doubt the seriousness of this thesis, and suspect that he simply wishes to appease 'the king' (the present rulers of China) in order to gain the king's ear and become his *consigliere*.

7. See the Gini coefficients of these countries. See data at: http://en.wikipedia.org/wiki/List_of_countries_by_income_equality; accessed 15 January 2012.

8. For a more detailed discussion of the Confucian hybrid regime, its merits, objections to it and responses to these objections, see Bai 2009b: ch. 3. For an earlier and partial version in English, see Bai 2008a.

9. Qian 1996 and 2005 contain more detailed historical accounts of these practices, along with insightful analyses.

10. The following discussion is a summary of parts of Bai 2008a and Bai 2009b: ch. 3.

11. See, for example, Ackerman and Fishkin 2004, 2005; and, more recently, Caplan 2008. For a more popular account, see Kristof 2008.

12. See, for example, Rawls 1996, 1999; and Ackerman and Fishkin 2004, 2005.

13. See, for example, Rawls 1996, 1999.

14. I have often received this reaction when discussing the idea of the Confucian hybrid regime.

FOUR

1. The translations of the *Lao Zi* in this book are mine. Alternatives are the complete translation of the *Lao Zi* in Chan 1969, and in Ivanhoe 2002.

2. The Chinese term for 'be told' is also *dao*; if this occurrence of *dao* were left untranslated, the text would read: 'The Dao that can *dao* is not the eternal Dao'.

3. The Chinese version is as follows: 读老子: 言者不知知者默, 此语吾闻于老君。若道老君是知者, 缘何自著五千文. It can be found in *The Complete Collection of Tang Poems* 全唐诗, Volume 455, no. 1. An online version is available at: www3.zzu.edu.cn/qtss/zzjpoem1.dll/viewoneshi?js=455&ns=001; accessed 8 January 2010.

4. You and *wu* are difficult to translate; 'being' and 'non-being' only partially catch their meanings. See Bai 2008c for detailed discussion.

5. Straw dogs are ceremonial objects that have a use during ceremonies, but are then discarded, with no further attention paid to them.

6. An interesting twist is found in the character Tang Seng 唐僧 in the classical Chinese novel Xi You Ji (*Journey to the West* 西游记), who is a Buddhist monk and symbolizes in the narrative someone who lacks the ability to distinguish between good and bad, and on account of this failing often ends up harming the good and exercising indiscriminate compassion for both the good and the bad. Tang Seng claims that a Buddhist monk worries about accidentally killing an ant when sweeping the floor (扫地恐伤蝼蚁命); he makes this claim when scolding a disciple who had apparently killed an agreeable old person, although this old person was actually an evil monster in disguise who wished to make an attempt on Tang Seng's life (*Journey to the West*: ch. 27).

7. What is considered natural and what is considered human are discussed in the next section.

8. The text of the above-quoted chapters in recently discovered and earlier versions of the *Lao Zi* (the *boshu* 帛书 and the *chujian* 楚简) tends to be less radical than the text of the received version. As indicated above, my references are to the received text. I do not consider the complicated textual issues involved in comparing the versions, except to say that the *Lao Zi*, and the text of the two chapters in question, would lack much of their force if only the *boshu* and *chujian* texts had survived.

9. It should be pointed out that in his later and far more comprehensive work (Liu 2006: 235–42, 398–405), Liu himself criticizes this misunderstanding, and points out similarities and subtle differences between understandings of non-action and naturalness in the *Lao Zi* and in Confucius, although I do not always agree with his judgements. He also insists that the idea of non-action was originally from the *Lao Zi* (Liu 2006: 236). The issue regarding the origin of the idea of non-action apparently depends upon the dating of the *Analects* and the *Lao Zi*, and therefore need not concern the reader.

10. The seat of the king is to face south. Thus the last line means that Shun did nothing but sit in a proper and respectful manner on his seat, instead of running around to fix things.

11. Confucius's own attitude towards heaven is sometimes ambivalent. For example, in the *Analects* 11.9, hearing about the untimely death of Yan Yuan 颜渊, arguably his best disciple, who could have kept faith with Confucius's ideas, 'Confucius said, "Alas! Heaven has killed me! Heaven has killed me!"' This passage indicates that heaven was unconcerned with human affairs, which disappointed Confucius. Thus, for Confucius, heaven is humane, but at the same time its humanity is beyond our understanding. Xun Zi explicitly claims: 'The operation of Heaven has its regularity. It does not exist for the sake of Yao [the sage-ruler], nor does it cease to exist because of Jie [the tyrant]' (*Xun Zi* Chapter 17). So, according to both Confucius and Xun Zi, we must

act without hoping that heaven will help in any way. We do our best, and let fate decide.

12. To be clear, calling this understanding descriptive does not mean that it has no normative implications. For example, one may loosen one's attachment to material goods and worldly glories on realizing that things come and go.

13. That is, not those who are forced into crimes by tyrannical and lustful rulers.

14. A similar idea is expressed in Chapter 58, the relevant passage from which is quoted and discussed above.

15. On this state being hypothetical rather than historical or factual, see, for example, Rousseau 1964: 103.

16. See Diamond 1999: 265–92; Wrangham 2004. Most shockingly, Wrangham points out that, during the twentieth century, Russia, Germany and Japan each experienced rates of war deaths that were less than half the average rate in pre-state hunter–gatherer societies (Wrangham 2004: 30). Incidentally, according to Diamond, the threshold below which everyone in a society can know everyone else is several hundred, and it is only in such a small society that conflict can be mediated without a separate authority. Beyond this threshold, violence can only be controlled effectively by a centralized authority with a monopoly of force (Diamond 1999: 286).

17. I emphasize the qualifications 'constructive' and 'as a whole' because I wish to leave room for acknowledging their powerful critiques of civilization.

18. For an alternative English translation, see Ames and Hall 2003: 201. For the original Chinese text, see Wang 1993: 302–6.

19. For an English translation, see Palmer 1996, 167–8; Graham 2001, 121.

FIVE

1. For the issues involved with the terms 'Legalism' and *fa*, see Goldin 2011. I do not always agree with his reservations regarding these terms. Some of the issues he raises are not necessarily particular to the Legalist school, but will arise whenever we try to group thinkers together into a school.

2. In other versions, the term for 'laws and edicts' is replaced with the term for 'good things' (Chen 2003: 281). But it is quite clear that, overall, the *Lao Zi* is against the conspicuous use of laws and regulations.

3. *Qing* can mean 'matter of fact' or 'emotions'. In this instance, it means 'matter of fact'.

4. Translations of the passages from the *Han Fei Zi* quoted in this book are mine. For alternative translations, see Liao 1939 (complete); Watson 1964 (incomplete but more recent).

5. See John Locke's insightful analysis of this issue (*The Second Treatise on Civil Government*: paras 46–48, in Locke 1986: 29–30).

6. The meanings of the Chinese characters 公 (*gong*) and 私 (*si*) have evolved over the years. They now refer to 'public' and 'private'. Some have argued against interpreting *gong* as 'public' and *si* as 'private'. There is no need to go into these debates here other than making the following clarifications. The interest of *gong* in the *Han Fei Zi* is often identified with the interest of the ruler. But, as I will argue, in the *Han Fei Zi* the interest of the ruler is often identified with the interest of the state. The question of whether the interest of the state is the same as the interest of the public has its own historical evolution. Some may object to my interpretation that for Han Fei Zi the interest of the ruler is identical with the interest of the state, and, from a contemporary point of view, some may argue that the state's interest should be that of all its people's interests combined, a view with which Han Fei Zi did not necessarily agree. I do not agree with the first objection, and consider the second objection as taking one interpretation of the public as the only one possible.

7. Guan Zhong was prime minister of the State of Qi during the Spring and Autumn period, who helped to make Qi the most powerful state at the time; he is said to have developed and practised some Legalist ideas.

8. 'Laws' is used here in the broad sense, and does not refer merely to the established laws of a state.

9. Again, this is not to deny the fundamental differences between the *Lao Zi* and Han Fei Zi and modern mainstream European economists. The commercial and industrial revolutions are unique to European modernity. Before these revolutions the Physiocrats, like Han Fei Zi, thought that the only truly productive economic activity was agricultural, and they looked down on commerce. Although Han Fei Zi tried to eliminate human factors from politics, he considered state authority essential, and a monopoly over state finance is part of this absolute authority. For example, as we will see, one of the five ways in which a ruler's power can be blocked is for the ministers to gain control of the wealth and the interests of the state. This is one reason that, in the famous policy debate on whether the government should have a monopoly over salt and iron (recorded in *The Discourses on Salt and Iron* 盐铁论), the Legalist voice is in favour of a state monopoly. However, it is interesting to speculate on whether Han Fei Zi would have favoured laissez-faire economics were he to have witnessed the industrialized world. My hunch is that he would.

10. 'Position' (shi 势) is a crucial concept in Han Fei Zi's political philosophy, the meaning of which it is difficult to convey. What he is trying to

say here is that the ideal ruler should rely upon what his position or office dictates, putting aside his own wisdom and virtues.

11. An interesting comparison is the alleged proclamation of Louis XIV, 'I am the state', during European modernization, thereby identifying the ruler with the state.

12. One might compare this with a similar objection raised to Socrates' construction of the beautiful city (*Republic* 419a–421c).

13. By 'effective control' here I don't mean the kind of suppression of liberties normal in a totalitarian state, but rather the state's ability to know what happens in even the furthest corner of the state and to react to it properly and legally. In the pre-industrialization and pre-information age, a rebellion could have been under way for some time before the central government heard about it, and yet in today's advanced societies a car accident on a remote section of a highway will be handled swiftly. Employing a distinction introduced by the British political theorist Michael Mann, I am concerned here with the 'infrastructural power of the state', defined as 'the ability of the state to actually penetrate civil society, and to implement logistically political decisions throughout the realm', and not about the 'despotic power' that rulers exercise to do things at their will (Mann 1988: 5). We can thus argue that Han Fei Zi himself confuses these two powers of the state. However, for Han Fei Zi, perhaps the only way to possess infrastructural power is for a ruler to wield despotic power, given that the means of communication were severely limited during his time.

14. There may have been other reasons. The sovereign power in modern democracies is the people, which helps to strengthen the unity and stability of the state.

15. See, for example, Goldin 2011.

SIX

1. A similar but perhaps less radical and less successful attempt to centralize power was made by Louis XIV, which again indicates similarities between European modernization and China's transition from the Eastern Zhou to the Qin dynasty.

2. Many historical works deal with the issues discussed in the last two paragraphs. See, for example, Fei 1998; Qian 2005; Yu 2004a, 2008.

3. Qian 1996 contains more detailed discussion of this issue.

4. For example, see Liu Zongyuan 柳宗元, *On Feudalism* 封建论; Wang Fuzhi 王夫之, *Reading Tongjian* 读通鉴论; Huang Zongxi 黄宗羲, *Ming Yi Dai Fang Lu* 明夷待访录; and Gu Yanwu 顾炎武, 'On Jun-Xian' 郡县论.

5. See Qian 2005 for a detailed historical account of this issue.

6. In this chapter, entitled 'Loyalty and Filial Piety', Han Fei Zi argues that if the sense of loyalty and filial piety is properly applied, it can

bolster the authority of the state. Here he seems to acknowledge the importance of certain values to the stability of the state, which partly answers the challenge that his system was based strictly upon reward and punishment. But how this use of values is to be reconciled with the teachings in other chapters of the *Han Fei Zi* that emphasize the use of only reward and punishment is unclear. It is also debatable whether this blind loyalty Han Fei Zi promotes can resist scrutiny to the same degree as the sincere loyalty that was cultivated through familial care, as early Confucians advocated.

7. See Qian 1996, 2005.
8. Considering the fact that the Chinese Communist Party was founded by the most radical among anti-tradition radicals, it is small wonder that some of the present leaders of China should misunderstand the nature of the Chinese regime.
9. See Qian 1996 and 2005 for more detailed discussion.
10. A recent attempt is that of the political theorist Zheng Yongnian 郑 永年, who argues that comparison with the Chinese emperorship is a better means to understand the Chinese Communist Party (CCP) than the concept of a political party in the Western sense (Zheng 2011). Using this analogy and my previous arguments, we can see the CCP as a Chinese emperor with far fewer checks and balances than those offered by Confucians in past regimes. Indeed, as suggested in the previous section, it is perhaps more productive to compare the CCP with emperors of the Qing dynasty than with previous traditional Chinese regimes, because both represent an alien invasion of China. In the Qing dynasty, in order to maintain their tight rule, every provincial post had to have a Manchurian lord 满大人 (Manchurian being the nationality of the Qing rulers). Similarly, in Communist China, every office has to have an executive and a 'party secretary' 党委书记.

CONCLUSION

1. See, for example, Fei 1998.
2. As Benjamin Elman has observed, the Chinese *ke ju* examination system (examining and awarding credentials but not educating those who took the exams) provided education on the cheap. See Elman 2000 for further details.

References

Ackerman, Bruce, and James Fishkin (2004), 'Righting the Ship of Democracy', *Legal Affairs*, January/February 2004: 34–9.
———— (2005), *Deliberation Day*. New Haven, CT: Yale University Press.
Ames, Roger T., and David L. Hall (trans.) (2003), *Daodejing*. New York: Ballantine Books.
Bai, Tongdong (2008a), 'A Mencian Version of Limited Democracy', *Res Publica*, vol. 14, no. 1, March: 19–34.
———— (2008b), 'Back to Confucius: A Comment on the Debate on the Confucian Idea of Consanguineous Affection', *Dao: A Journal of Comparative Philosophy*, vol. 7, no. 1, March, 2008: 27–33.
———— (2008c), 'An Ontological Interpretation of You (something) (有) and Wu (Nothing) (无) in the *Laozi*', *Journal of Chinese Philosophy*, vol. 35, no. 2, June: 339–51.
———— (2009a), 'The Price of Serving Meat – On Confucius's and Mencius's Views of Human and Animal Rights', *Asian Philosophy*, vol. 19, no. 1, March: 85–99.
———— (2009b), *The New Mission of an Old State: The Contemporary and Comparative Relevance of Classical Confucian Political Philosophy* 旧邦新命: 古今中西参照下的古典儒家政治哲学. Beijing: Peking University Press. (Revised English edition forthcoming.)
———— (2009c), 'How to Rule without Taking Unnatural Actions (无为而治): A Comparative Study of the Political Philosophy of the *Laozi*', *Philosophy East and West*, vol. 59, no. 4, October: 481–502.
———— (2011), 'Preliminary Remarks: Han Fei Zi – First Modern Political Philosopher?', *Journal of Chinese Philosophy*, vol. 38, no. 1, March: 4–13.

Bell, Daniel (2006), *Beyond Liberal Democracy*. Princeton, NJ: Princeton University Press.

───── (2008), *China's New Confucianism*. Princeton, NJ: Princeton University Press.

Bell, Daniel, and Hahm Chaibong (2003), *Confucianism for the Modern World*. Cambridge: Cambridge University Press.

Bentham, Jeremy (1949), *An Introduction to the Principles of Morals and Legislation*. New York: Hafner Press.

Bloom, Allan (trans.) (1991), *The Republic of Plato*. New York: Basic Books.

Brooks, David (2010), 'The Power Elite', *New York Times*, 19 February.

Caplan, Bryan (2008), *The Myth of the Rational Voter: Why Democracies Choose Bad Policies*. Princeton, NJ: Princeton University Press.

Chan, Sin Yee (2003), 'The Confucian Conception of Gender in the Twenty-first Century,' in Daniel Bell and Hahm Chaibong, *Confucianism for the Modern World*. Cambridge: Cambridge University Press, pp. 312–33.

Chan, Wing-Tsit (1969), *A Source Book in Chinese Philosophy*. Princeton, NJ: Princeton University Press.

Chen, Guying 陈鼓应 (2003), *A Contemporary Commentary and Translation of the Lao Zi* 老子今注今译, rev. edn. Beijing: Shangwu Yinshuguan.

Chen, Qiyou 陈奇猷 (2000), *Han Feizi, with New Collations and Commentary* 韩非子新校注. Shanghai: Shanghai Guji.

Cheng, Hao 程颢, and Cheng Yi 程颐 (1992), *Surviving Works of the Two Cheng's and Additional Works of the Two Cheng's* 二程遗书与二程外书. Shanghai: Shanghai Guji.

Cheng, Shude 程树德 (1990), *Collected Commentaries on the Analects* 论语集解. Beijing: Zhonghua Shuju.

Csiksentmihalyi, Mark, and Philip J. Ivanhoe (eds) (1999), *Religious and Philosophical Aspects of the Laozi*. Albany, NY: State University of New York Press.

Davidson, Adam (2012), 'Come on, China, Buy Our Stuff', *New York Times*, 25 January.

Diamond, Jared (1999), *Guns, Germs, and Steel*. New York: W.W. Norton.

Elman, Benjamin (2000), *A Cultural History of Civil Examinations in Late Imperial China*. Berkeley: University of California Press.

Fei, Xiaotong 费孝通 (1998), *Rural China and Institutions of Child-Birth and Child-Rearing* 乡土中国 生育制度. Beijing: Peking University Press.

Fukuyama, Francis (1992), *The End of History and the Last Man*, New York: Avon Books.

───── (2011), *The Origins of Political Order: From Prehuman Times to the French Revolution*. New York: Farrar, Straus & Giroux.

Fung, Yu-lan 冯友兰 (1966), *A Short History of Chinese Philosophy*. New York: Free Press.

Gan, Yang (甘阳), (2007), *Synthesizing Three Traditions* 通三统. Beijing: Sanlian Press.

Goldin, Paul (2011), 'Persistent Misconceptions about Chinese "Legalism"', *Journal of Chinese Philosophy*, vol. 38, no. 1, March: 88–104.

Graham, A.C. (2001), *Chuang-Tsŭ: The Inner Chapters*. Indianapolis: Hackett.

Han, Dongyu 韩东育 (2003), *Studies of Japanese Neo-Legalists of More Recent Times* 《日本近世新法家研究》. Beijing: Zhonghua Shuju.

Hobson, John M. (2004), *The Eastern Origins of Western Civilization*. Cambridge: Cambridge University Press.

Hui, Victorial Tin-Bor (2005), *War and State Formation in Ancient China and Early Modern Europe*. Cambridge: Cambridge University Press.

Ivanhoe, Philip J. (1999), 'The Concept of *de* ('Virtue') in the *Laozi*', in Mark Csiksentmihalyi and Philip J. Ivanhoe (eds), *Religious and Philosophical Aspects of the Laozi*. Albany, NY: State University of New York Press, pp. 239–57.

———— (2002), *The Daodejing of Laozi*. Indianapolis: Hackett.

Jaspers, Karl (1953), *The Origin and Goal of History*, trans. Michael Bullock. London: Routledge & Kegan Paul.

Jiao, Xun 焦循 (1986), *Mengzi Zhengyi* 孟子正义, collected in *Zhuzi Jiecheng* 诸子集成. Shanghai: Shanghai Shudian.

Johnston, Alastair Iain (1998), *Cultural Realism: Strategic Culture and Grand Strategy in Chinese History*. Princeton, NJ: Princeton University Press.

Kant, Immanuel (1998), *Groundwork of the Metaphysics of Morals.*, trans. Mary Gregor. Cambridge: Cambridge University Press.

Kissinger, Henry (2011), *On China*. London: Penguin.

Kohn, Livia, and Michael LaFargue (eds) (1998), *Lao-tzu and the Tao-te-ching*. Albany, NY: State University of New York Press.

Kristof, Nicholas D. (2005), 'I have a Nightmare', *New York Times*, 12 March.

———— (2008), 'With a Few More Brains', *New York Times*, 30 March.

Lau, D.C. 刘殿爵 (trans.) (1963), *Tao Te Ching*. Baltimore, MD: Penguin.

———— (2000), *Confucius: The Analects*. Hong Kong: Chinese University Press.

———— (2003), *Mencius*, rev. bilingual edn. Hong Kong: Chinese University Press.

Li, Chenyang (ed.) (2000), *The Sage and the Second Sex: Confucianism, Ethics, and Gender*. Chicago: Open Court.

Liao, W.K. (trans.) (1939), *The Complete Works of Han Fei Tzu*. London: Arthur Probsthain.

Liu, An 刘安 (1986), *Huai Nan Zi*, collected in *Zhuzi Jiecheng* 诸子集成. Shanghai: Shanghai Shudian.

Liu, Xiaogan 刘笑敢 (1998), 'Naturalness (Tzu-jan), the Core Value in Taoism: Its Ancient Meaning and Its Significance Today', in Livia Kohn and Michael

LaFargue (eds), *Lao-tzu and the Tao-te-ching*. Albany, NY: State University of New York Press, pp. 211–28.

——— (2006), *Lao Zi Gujin* 老子古今. Beijing: Chinese Academy of Social Sciences Press.

Locke, John (1986), *The Second Treatise on Civil Government*. New York: Prometheus Books.

Maddison, Augus (2006), *The World Economy: A Millenial Perspective*. Paris: Organization for Economic Cooperation and Development.

Makeham, John (2008), *Lost Soul: 'Confucianism' in Contemporary Chinese Academic Discourse*. Cambridge, MA: Harvard University Asia Center.

Mann, Michael (1988), *States, War and Capitalism*. Oxford: Blackwell.

Nietzsche, Friedrich (1954), *Thus Spoke Zarathustra*, trans. Walter Kaufmann. Harmondsworth: Penguin.

——— (1994), *On the Genealogy of Morality*, ed. Keith Ansell-Pearson, trans. Carol Diethe. Cambridge: Cambridge University Press.

——— (2002), *Beyond Good and Evil*, ed. Rolf-Peter Horstmann and Judith Norman, trans. Judith Norman. Cambridge: Cambridge University Press.

Nisbett, Richard (2003), *The Geography of Thought: How Asians and Westerners Think Differently ... and Why*. New York: Free Press.

Ortega y Gasset, José (1932), *The Revolt of the Masses*. New York: W.W. Norton.

Palmer, Martin (1996), *The Book of Chuantzu*. London: Arkana, Penguin Books.

Pollak, Michael (1998), *Mandarins, Jews, and Missionaries: The Jewish Experience in the Chinese Empire*. New York: Weatherhill.

Puett, Michael (1998), 'China in Early Eurasian History: A Brief Review of Scholarship on the Issue', in Victor Mair (ed.), *The Bronze Age and Early Iron Age Peoples of Eastern Central Asia*. Washington DC: Institute for the Study of Man, pp. 699–715.

Qian Mu 钱穆 (1996), *Outlines of the History of China* 国史大纲. Beijing: Shangwu Press.

——— (2005), *Merits and Problems of Chinese Politics of the Past Dynasties* 中国历代政治得失. Beijing: Sanlian Shudian.

Rawls, John (1971), *A Theory of Justice*. Cambridge, MA: Harvard University Press.

——— (1996), *Political Liberalism*. New York: Columbia University Press.

——— (1999), *The Law of Peoples, with 'The Idea of Public Reason Revisited'*. Cambridge, MA: Harvard University Press.

Roetz, Heiner (1993), *Confucian Ethics of the Axial Age*. Albany, NY: SUNY Press.

Rousseau, Jean-Jacques (1964), *The First and Second Discourses*, trans. Roger D. and Judith R. Masters. New York: St. Martin's Press.

———— (1978), *On the Social Contract with Geneva Manuscript and Political Economy*. ed. Roger D. Masters, trans. Judith R. Masters. New York: St. Martin's Press.

Schwartz, Benjamin (1985), *The World of Thought in Ancient China*. Cambridge, MA: Belknap Press of Harvard University Press.

Shapiro, Sidney (ed. and trans.) (1984), *Jews in Old China: Studies by Chinese Scholars*. New York: Hippocrene Books.

Shi, Tianjian (2011), *The Logic of Politics in Mainland China and Taiwan: A Cultural Basis of Attitudes and Behavior*. Cambridge: Cambridge University Press.

Shi, Tianjian, and Jie Lu (2010), 'The Meaning of Democracy: The Shadow of Confucianism', *Journal of Democracy*, vol. 21, no. 4, October: 123–9.

Sima, Qian 司马迁 (1981), *Shiji* 史记 (*The Records of the Grand Historian*), in *Twenty Five Historical Records* 二十五史. Shanghai: Shanghai Guji Press.

Tang, Junyi 唐君毅 (1996), *Classics of Contemporary Chinese Scholarship: The Tang Junyi Volume*, ed. Liu Mengxi 刘梦溪. Shi Jia Zhuang: Hebei Education Press.

Tu, Weiming 杜维明 (1996), *Confucian Tradition in East Asian Modernity*. Cambridge, MA: Harvard University Press.

Vogel, Ezra (1979), *Japan as Number One: Lessons for America*. Cambridge, MA: Harvard University Press.

Wang, Bi 王弼 (1991), *Lao Zi's Dao De Jing with Wang Bi's Commentaries* 老子道德经 – 王弼注, collected in *Zhuzi Jicheng* 诸子集成. Shanghai: Shanghai Shudian.

Wang, Ka 王卡 (ed.) (1993), *Lao Zi Dao De Jing He Shang Gong Zhang Ju* 老子道德经河上公章句. Beijing: Zhonghua Shuju.

Wang, Robin R. (ed.) (2003), *Images of Women in Chinese Thought and Culture*. Indianapolis: Hackett.

Wang, Su 王肃 (ed.) (1990), *Sayings of Confucius's School* 孔子家语. Shanghai: Shanghai Guji.

Wang, Yangming 王阳明 (1992), *The Complete Works of Wang Yangming* 王阳明全集. Shanghai: Shanghai Guji.

Wang, Yuan-kang (2011), *Harmony and War: Confucian Culture and Chinese Power Politics*. New York: Columbia University Press.

Watson, Burton (trans.) (1964), *Han Fei Tzu: Basic Writings*. New York: Columbia University Press.

Weber, Max (1958), *The Protestant Ethic and the Spirit of Capitalism*, trans. Talcott Parsons. New York: Charles Scribner's Sons.

———— (1968), *Religion of China*, trans. Hans H. Gerth. New York: Free Press.

Wrangham, Richard (2004), 'Killer Species', *Dædalus*, Fall 2004: 25–35.

Xu, Xin (2003), *The Jews of Kaifeng, China*. Jersey City, NJ: KTAV.

Yu, Yingshi 余英时 (2004a), *The Historical World of Zhu Xi – Studies of the Political Culture of Song Scholar-Officials* 朱熹的历史世界 – 宋代士大夫政治文化研究. Beijing: Sanlian.

————— (2004b), *The Tradition of Chinese Thought and Its Modern Transformation* 中国思想传统及其现代变迁. Guilin: Guangxi Normal University Press.

————— (2008), 'I and the Contemporary Studies of the History of Chinese Thoughts' 我与中国现代思想史研究, *Si Xiang* 思想, vol. 8, January: 1–18.

Zakaria, Fareed (2003), *The Future of Freedom: Illiberal Democracy at Home and Abroad.* New York: W.W. Norton.

Zhang, Zai 张载 (1978), *The Collected Works of Zhang Zai* 张载集. Beijing: Zhonghua Shuju.

Zheng, Yongnian 郑永年 (2011), *The Chinese Communist Party as Organizational Emperor: Culture, Reproduction, and Transformation.* New York: Routledge.

Index

Sage-rulers, 17, 108, 125–7, 132; ideal,
    63; requirements of, 62
SAWS (Spring and Autumn and
    Warring States) era, 16, 94, 102,
    177; brutal wars, 49; changes
    during, 17; transitions, 19
scholar-officials, 165–6
Schwartz, Benjamin, 103, 107, 110
secularization, 25
'self-sufficiency', 68, 108
sexual desire, 104
Shang dynasty, 154; King Tang, 17;
    kings, 29
Shang Yang (Lord Shang) (Gongsun
    Yang), 113–17, 119–20, 140
Shen Buhai, 118
Shen Nong, 67
Shiji, 83, 114, 118, 121
Shu Qi, 154
Shun, sage-ruler, 17, 62–3, 72, 75–6,
    93, 132
Sima Qian, 121; Shiji, 30
simpler life, return to calls, 111
slave morality, 34
slavery, Ancient Greece, 79
social glue, 21, 33–4, 39, 123–4, 179;
    feudalism, 31; humanity as, 43,
    85; need for, 28; problem of, 10
society of strangers, 177–8
Socrates, 58, 73, 139; human
    ignorance conception, 89
soft power, 45
'Solitary Indignation', 154
Song dynasty, 165, 170
South Korea, 71; Confucian heritage,
    70
Southeast Asia, financial crisis
    1997–98, 2
sovereigns, legitimacy, 151–2, 172–3,
    177, see also rulers
Spring and Autumn period, 13, 16,
    18; wars, 20
stability, 152
state(s): as big family, 41;
    authoritarian, 172; city, 40; ideal
    small, 106, 112, 150; large, 103;
    Legalistic, 158; modern European,
    181; monopoly of violence, 116;
    size importance, 78; small, 122,

139; weak, 138
'subtle light' tactics, 108
Tang dynasty, 165, 167–8, 170
Tasmanians, 106–7
technologies, 102; communication
    and transportation, 103
Teng, Duke Wen of, 49, 50, 67
thought, pluralism, 132
Tibet: hippy idealization, 107; people
    of, 46; temples destroyed, 4;
    Western media coverage, 3
tolerance, 181
totalitarian control, 171–2
traditional political philosophy, 5–8,
    14, 176
tyrannical king, justified removals,
    135

universal love, ideal of, 37
urbanization, radical, 3
USA (United States of America), 2;
    conservatives, 40; economic
    inequality, 70–71; Iraq
    invasion, 86; meritocratic, 168;
    national identity, 46; natives
    extermination, 45; populism, 80;
    second Iraq attack, 51
utopia: pre-modern, 104
Uyghurs, 46

values: moral, 161; pluralism, 21, 152,
    161, 181; public, 182
violence, ethnic, 78
virtues, 144
Vogel, Ezra, 2

Wang Bi, 84, 108
Wang Mang, 165
Wang Yangming, 38
war(s), 100–101; causes, 125;
    Confucian caution, 47; Confucian
    type justification, 86; 'just', 46;
    of liberation, 50; theories of, 138;
    types, 52
Warring States period, 16, 18, 38,
    108, 110, 112, 138; savagery of, 20
wealth, concentration of, 103
Weber, Max, 2, 24, 27
Wei Yang, 115

About Zed Books

Zed Books is a critical and dynamic publisher, committed to increasing awareness of important international issues and to promoting diversity, alternative voices and progressive social change. We publish on politics, development, gender, the environment and economics for a global audience of students, academics, activist and general readers. Run as a co-operative, we aim to operate in an ethical and environmentally sustainable way.

Find out more at
www.zedbooks.co.uk

For up-to-date news, articles, reviews
and events information visit
http://zed-books.blogspot.com

To subscribe to the monthly Zed Books e-newsletter
send an email headed 'subscribe' to marketing@zedbooks.net

We can also be found on Facebook, ZNet,
Twitter and Library Thing.